SOUL-CENTRED

ALSO BY SARAH McLEAN

SOUL-CENTRED

TRANSFORM YOUR LIFE IN 8 WEEKS WITH MEDITATION

SARAH McLEAN

HAY HOUSE

Australia • Canada • Hong Kong • India
South Africa • United Kingdom • United States

First published and distributed in the United Kingdom by:
Hay House UK Ltd, 292B Kensal Rd, London W10 5BE. Tel.: (44) 20 8962 1230;
Fax: (44) 20 8962 1239. www.hayhouse.co.uk

Published and distributed in the United States of America by:
Hay House, Inc., PO Box 5100, Carlsbad, CA 92018-5100. Tel.: (1) 760 431 7695 or
(800) 654 5126; Fax: (1) 760 431 6948 or (800) 650 5115. www.hayhouse.com

Published and distributed in Australia by:
Hay House Australia Ltd, 18/36 Ralph St, Alexandria NSW 2015.
Tel.: (61) 2 9669 4299; Fax: (61) 2 9669 4144. www.hayhouse.com.au

Published and distributed in the Republic of South Africa by:
Hay House SA (Pty), Ltd, PO Box 990, Witkoppen 2068. Tel./Fax: (27) 11 467
8904. www.hayhouse.co.za

Published and distributed in India by:
Hay House Publishers India, Muskaan Complex, Plot No.3, B-2, Vasant Kunj,
New Delhi – 110 070. Tel.: (91) 11 4176 1620; Fax: (91) 11 4176 1630.
www.hayhouse.co.in

Distributed in Canada by:
Raincoast, 9050 Shaughnessy St, Vancouver, BC V6P 6E5. Tel.: (1) 604 323 7100;
Fax: (1) 604 323 2600

Design: Tricia Breidenthal

A catalogue record for this book is available from the British Library.

ISBN 978-1-84850-780-7

Printed and bound in Great Britain by CPI Group (UK) Ltd, Croydon, CR0 4YY.

For you, the explorer

CONTENTS

PREFACE

Meditation can transform your life. I know this because it transformed my life and the lives of many of my students and friends. As they set off on their meditation paths, they noticed that not only did they feel more relaxed and peaceful, but their constant companions of apathy, discomfort, and anxiety soon transformed into inspiration, comfort, and joy. They felt more engaged and purposeful, and their entire relationship to life was transformed.

When I began my own daily meditation practice in the late 1980s, I had no idea what was in store for me. Back then I looked like I was on the right track as a successful career woman, but I didn't feel that way. Instead, I felt dissatisfied. I longed for a purpose, I longed for love, and I longed for a meaningful life. When I turned to meditation, I had no idea that this simple practice would give me the gifts I was looking for. I learned how to become aware of the moment at hand, how to quickly return to peace after being upset, to see things clearly rather than habitually, to be kind to myself, to say what I mean, and to focus my attention on what matters. I developed genuine confidence, stability, creativity, and compassion for myself as well as all beings. I noticed the interconnectedness of the universe and felt a renewed wonder for life. Meditation served to change my perspective on *everything*.

Perhaps these changes seem nebulous and out of reach for you, but rest assured, they are possible. I've taught thousands of people to meditate, including FBI agents, judges, professional athletes, teachers, students, lawyers, engineers, brain surgeons, CEOs, teens, retirees, Republicans, Democrats, Christians, Jews, Hindus, Muslims, Buddhists, atheists, and agnostics. They all, like me, found their lives transformed through meditation—so much so that, in some cases, they have found a vibrancy, health, and satisfaction beyond anything they ever dared to imagine.

The meditation training program I offer in this book is decidedly mainstream. Even though I've immersed myself in the studies of world religions, exploring mystical or esoteric concepts and practices, I wanted to use this book to make what I learned accessible to everyone. There's no need for anyone to change their religion, adopt new beliefs, spend time in some cloistered community, or even learn a new vocabulary in order to understand and practice meditation.

And while many receive very practical benefits from meditation, there is a spiritual aspect to it as well. Meditation makes possible a *soul-centered* life: a life you live from your own unique and peaceful center, your own soul. Each one of us has the ability to live life peacefully, powerfully, authentically, and with compassion. I am dedicated to sharing what I know to help you become peaceful and soul-centered through meditation. If each one of us finds peace, then together we can make this world a sweeter place for all beings.

◗ ◖

The contrast between my childhood and teen years to my adult life perfectly illustrates the power of meditation to create transformation. If my life could shift so dramatically, then anyone's can. As a young girl, I was sensitive and artistic; I related better to animals and nature than to people. My father, though bright and funny, was explosive and difficult to live with. My mother, though smart and pretty, was emotionally removed and became an alcoholic. Although I felt love for everyone, I also felt disconnected and alone. I was often in tears at home and at school, and felt like a "bad girl." As an adolescent, I lived up to my bad-girl persona and became a defiant, boy-crazy thrill seeker. At 17, I dropped out of high school and left home. My life quickly took another turn, and I joined the military when I was 18.

Ten years later, I was a successful real estate agent living in Washington, D.C. By then, I had been a behavioral specialist in the U.S. Army; eloped with and gotten divorced from a violent felon; earned my college degree; and explored Europe, Turkey, Pakistan, and Thailand by bicycle. Throughout that decade I'd tried many conventional and not-so-conventional ways to answer the questions, *Who am I? Why am I here?* and *How can I be happy?* But even in my late 20s and having "made it," I still couldn't shake the question, *What is my life about?* I had some vague sense that the answer would come someday, but I was confused and didn't know where my future would lead.

I soon experienced what some might call a "dark night of the soul." I became depressed and inconsolable, and felt that I didn't want to live the life I was living. I didn't know where to turn. The old way wasn't working, but I didn't know how to start something new. I realized I was having a spiritual crisis. For weeks I cried, prayed, read, and went for long, long walks. Eventually I was pointed toward meditation. It snapped me out of it. Quite soon after learning to meditate and adopting a daily meditation practice, I decided to leave everything I knew behind—my job, my house, my roommates and friends in Washington—and drove off with my cat to Florida to live a simple life by the beach. I wanted and needed to be in peace.

A few months later, Dr. Deepak Chopra, author of some of the books I'd been reading to get me through my crisis, came to Fort Lauderdale for a public talk. I went to hear him, and, as he spoke about ancient wisdom and mind-body health, I tingled from head to toe. I immediately knew I needed to further immerse myself in the natural healing practices and lifestyle he described. His ideas defied conventional Western ideas of health and disease and offered a new perspective: *health is more than just being free from disease; it is a dynamic state of balance and integration of mind, body, and spirit.* This isn't a unique concept nowadays, but in 1990, it was a completely new paradigm. I called the Maharishi Ayurveda Health Center in Lancaster, Massachusetts, where Deepak had his practice. After a few conversations with the director, I was invited to come live and work at the center.

I joined the 15 others who lived on-site, and settled into my own tiny room above the industrial kitchen. It was in a wing of the mansion next to where the guests stayed for weeklong detoxification and healing programs. In exchange for training, food, lodging, and a small stipend, I worked six days a week, answering phones and talking to people who, like me, had read Deepak's books and wanted to know more. During the years I lived and worked there, I studied the ancient healing science of Ayurveda and learned a variety of advanced meditation techniques. My meditation periods increased from 20 minutes to almost 60 minutes twice a day. My mind was clear, my body felt good, and I felt like I was on the right path.

A couple of years later, Deepak was invited to head a mind-body health center in Southern California in conjunction with a major health-care facility. I joined him there and over the next eight years I taught meditation and mind-body health programs and served as The Chopra Center's program director. I helped train the staff, teach the guests, and manage the team of educators.

Then, one day, as I sat with my co-workers in a staff meeting, I knew in my heart that it was time to leave. I wanted to explore even more. I left for India to discover the roots of meditation, Ayurveda, and to explore the mystical. I spent six months there, mostly at a traditional Hindu ashram in Kerala in southern India, where I meditated, did yoga, and chanted for many hours a day. I also spent time in Dharamsala in northern India, teaching English to the Tibetan Buddhist nuns, as part of the Dalai Lama's plan for them to go into the world and educate others. I had journeyed into another world, and I was not ready to go home when my visa expired.

On my return to the States, nothing seemed important to me except my quest for expanded awareness. I missed living in a meditation community as I had been doing, so I became a resident at the Yokoji Zen Mountain Center in the San Jacinto Mountains outside of Idyllwild, California. The training was intensive; during certain periods, we would sit in meditation for up to eight hours a day. Even when we weren't sitting, meditation was a part of every activity as we mindfully worked, walked, and ate our meals.

After almost two years at the Zen Center I felt ready to integrate stillness and mindfulness into my life in the "real world." I was hired to work with Gary Zukav, author of *The Seat of the Soul,* and then went to work for Byron Katie, the woman who founded the inquiry process called The Work. I eventually landed in Sedona, Arizona, the place I now call home.

○ ○

As I look back, it's apparent that, although I'd made some unusual decisions as a young woman, I wasn't the "bad girl" I'd thought I was. Instead, I'd been like a lost child who had to find her own path, who had to learn to trust her inner wisdom. With the practice of meditation, I was able to get rid of much of the stress that had accumulated in my body and mind from my past. As the stress lessened and my mind quieted, I could connect to my inner wisdom. I learned to trust it. My inner wisdom, like yours, is similar to a reliable GPS that always has my best interests in mind, as well as those of others. It continues to lead me to teachers and experiences to help me see more clearly and to love myself and the world.

My life has permanently transformed—from one of suffering, fear, chaos, and running away . . . to one in which I regularly experience a deep, true inner peace that I can return to again and again. Today, I feel truly loved and supported by life, and live in a world that is friendly.

My transformation unfolded slowly and steadily after I began my daily practice of meditation. In this book, I'll share with you what I learned in order to transform my life; and in case you're wondering—*no*, you don't have to run off to India or live in a monastery to learn how to meditate. You can sit right where you are and get it all.

○ ○ ○

INTRODUCTION

Most of us aren't trained for the journey inward to the very seat of our soul, and most are not sure how or where to begin. In fact, we are conditioned to pay attention to external phenomena, and this keeps us unaware that an inner world even exists. Your body and its sensory apparatus are trained to focus your attention on the world *out there*, not on inner experiences. You navigate your way through life with your senses: seeing, feeling, hearing, tasting, and smelling the world.

Your attention is drawn outward, and you label that which is around you. Then you describe yourself by referring to those external things whether they are objects, relationships, places, situations, or experiences. Perhaps you see yourself the way some of your friends and family see you: as the sum total of your various positions, possessions, relationships, and responsibilities in life. Perhaps you describe yourself by sharing your age, race, religion, or political party; where you live or where you grew up; what you used to do or plan to do; or your thoughts and feelings. But do all of those references add up to describe the *real* you?

The physical world exists in time and space and is constantly changing. Your physical body illustrates this perfectly. Look at a photo of yourself from ten years ago. Now look in the mirror— your physical form is probably very different today. Although you may not be aware that physical change is happening, it is. For example, your body constantly replaces old cells with new ones at the rate of millions per second. Can you really say you are your body when millions of your cells have already come and gone just as you were reading this sentence?

Your thoughts are pretty dynamic, too. Thousands of thoughts pass through your head each day, like *What am I going to have for dinner? I should call my mother, I'm thirsty,* or *How can I help them?* You also have a variety of feelings and emotions as a response to what you think or experience, and they too are always changing. So, you are not your thoughts, feelings, or emotions either. Your body and its sensations, the content of your thoughts, and the emotions you experience are all a *part* of you, but they are not the *whole* of you. Who you are is beyond all that.

Who Are You?

The real you is that part of you that has been with you since the day you were born. Some people call it your soul, your essence, or your presence. It doesn't matter what you call it, but it's important to know it's the aspect of you that doesn't change while everything else around you does. The real you is the one who is aware of your ever-changing body and calls it *home*. The real you is the one who witnesses, experiences, or observes your thoughts, feelings, actions and experiences. When you say, "I am feeling happy," who is the *I*? The *I* is that awareness beyond the thought. It's the real you. Your body, thoughts, and emotions are only the expression of that *I*.

Take a moment to turn your attention to the one who is reading this page. *You.* Keep reading, but notice where your attention is coming from, what the source of it is. Who is looking through your eyes? Just be with this experience for a moment.

You may have, for an instant, become aware of your own presence. It's a clear and simple awareness. And though now you might be aware of this presence for only a fleeting moment, after practicing meditation regularly you will create a deeper intimacy with and connection to this essential part of yourself. It's stable, wise, ever present, and dependable. Through meditation, this, your soul, becomes your reference point by which you navigate life; it's an inner compass that transforms the way you see yourself and the way you respond to the world. I call this being *soul-centered*. Although subtle, it will be a powerful life-changing shift for you.

Undoing the Stress

You are born full of energy and excitement. You are a joyous, peaceful, creative, energetic, present, connected, and loving being. These are qualities of your presence, your true nature. Why don't most of us experience ourselves in this way? This is because as we get older, stress from a variety of sources accumulates in our nervous system. And if we don't get rid of it, it can begin to mask our awareness of that joyous, peaceful aspect of ourselves.

The effects of stress over time are like a veil that hides the radiance of your true self, your soul's expression in the world. You can't go through life completely avoiding stress—it's just not possible. Fortunately, meditation is one of the most effective ways of reducing stress and its effects. Not only does meditation help you become more aware of what is actually causing you stress so you can avoid or change it, it also reduces the physical effects of stress on the mind and body. It connects you to who you really are.

Without the effects of stress, you are balanced and peaceful, and don't get easily triggered by external factors. This is what I mean by being soul-centered—you maintain a connection to the deepest part of you, the part of you that is clear, peaceful, and aware in each moment; and you develop the flexibility to easily return to this center, even after a disturbance. When you are soul-centered, you respond to life with wisdom, creativity, and confidence.

The Science Is In

I know from experience that people's lives are transformed by practicing meditation, and I'm happy when the science confirms it. Over decades, there have been hundreds of studies on the effects of meditation that confirm meditators regularly experience some terrific benefits as compared to non-meditators, including better health, greater intuition, increased mental focus, improved memory, decreased reactivity to stress, and fewer visits to a doctor. Researchers confirm that meditators have lowered cholesterol, decreased anxiety and depression, lessened ADHD symptoms, normalized blood sugar, improved mood, increased fertility, increased happiness, and reduced stress. They've shown that meditation can help you sleep better, enhance your immunity, and reduce chronic pain.

Some of the most exciting new research suggests that meditation can actually help you experience more peace, freedom, compassion (including self-compassion), creativity, connectedness, and awareness of the present moment. This happens because meditation can change the physical structure of your brain.

To understand how radical these findings are, you have to realize that only recently have scientists come to accept that the brain can change at all after someone reaches 25 to 30 years of age. It had been the conventional view that the brain finished developing around that age and remained stable during adulthood, then went downhill from there. I remember being told as a kid that I only had a limited number of brain cells, and so I should avoid activities that would compromise what I had. But today, as confirmed by studies of brain scans (including those of people who practice meditation), scientists accept the brain's ability to continue to grow, change, and become more flexible—known as *neuroplasticity*.

In the January 2011 issue of *Psychiatry Research: Neuroimaging*, researchers from Massachusetts General Hospital found that after only eight weeks of meditation for an average of 27 minutes a day, new meditators showed beneficial changes in their gray matter, the physical structure of their brains. Not only that, but these changes lasted long after the meditation period was over.

After only eight weeks of meditation, participants reported feeling less stressed, and researchers identified a correlating decrease in the gray matter of the amygdala—the area of the brain associated with the fight-or-flight response, anxiety, and stress. There was also an increase in gray matter in the hippocampus, an area of the brain known to be important for learning and memory. These changes would allow a person to be more empathetic and less emotionally reactive when faced with a challenge.

It doesn't take a scientific study to know that meditators feel less stress, more peace, equanimity, and an enhanced sense of well-being. In fact, these effects have been recorded in the earliest texts on yoga and meditation in India, China, and Japan. Modern-day brain imaging, it seems, is now catching up with what ancient wisdom has been saying all along: meditation helps you live a peaceful, fulfilling, soul-centered life.

What It Means to Be Soul-Centered

I came up with the term *soul-centered* to describe a particular shift in perspective: a transformation of the vantage point for one's life. It's a great way to live each day.

When you're soul-centered, you are not dependent on others for your sense of self or worthiness. Instead, you are guided by an inner reference point—your own soul. You are open to all possibilities and approach life courageously and fearlessly, without resistance or clinging, offensiveness or defensiveness. You can focus your attention where and when you want to, easily and without distraction. You have a receptive awareness and your natural state is relaxed, calm, peaceful, and loving toward yourself and others.

When you are soul-centered, your attention is in the present moment, receiving the moment, welcoming it. You accept things as they are. You don't struggle against what is happening now or at any time. You realize that you are safe and loved, no matter what. You become aware of a spacious quality in the present moment in which you can listen to your inner wisdom, make nourishing choices, feel your feelings fully, and take time to choose a response rather than react automatically to the world.

You have a deep inner wisdom and knowingness, make decisions easily, and are confident as you journey on your own path. What you think, feel, say, and do are integrated and in alignment with your deepest truth. You know when to say yes and when to say no; and in this way, you address each moment with integrity.

When you are soul-centered, your nervous system is stable yet flexible; no matter what occurs in life, you can handle it. If for some reason you are thrown off balance by a thought, experience, or difficult emotion, you quickly realize it and are easily able to regain your center point of peace.

You trust yourself and feel safe and confident wherever you go and whatever you do, no matter who does or does not approve of you, what anyone thinks about you, or what they say you should or shouldn't do. You are the self-sufficient navigator of your own path, yet you feel interconnected with all beings. You have compassion for all. You feel in communion with life and enjoy nature's support, sensing the love that surrounds you—the love that makes up *you*. You may feel closer to God, the creator, or the universe.

When you are soul-centered, you radiate the qualities of your soul. You are vital and clear, and have access to unbounded energy and creativity. The peace and silence of the soul is nourishing to your nervous system, and when you are soul-centered your very presence is nourishing to others. When I'm around soul-centered people, I notice they have a quiet power. They seem happy for no particular reason and radiate joy, harmony, health, integrity, and wholeness. They are authentic, loving, receptive, and present; they naturally draw others to them, creating situations and circumstances that support their desires.

How do you become soul-centered? The best way I've found is through the practice of meditation.

The 8-Week Program

The program in this book is based on my own journey through meditation. Each of the 8 weeks is centered around a theme, an ingredient of a soul-centered life. At the heart of the program are two primary meditation techniques derived from ancient practices: the sitting and mantra meditations. These techniques are what I and many of my students use in our everyday meditation routines.

You'll read stories that illustrate the challenges I met and the insights I discovered along the path of transformation, as well as stories from my students describing how their lives have changed. Each week you'll learn meditation practices and awareness exercises to help you fully embody the lesson. By following the program, you'll reduce stress, increase your self-awareness, and live a more fulfilling life as you become more:

- Engaged in the moment at hand, and alert to the choices you can make in each moment

- Spontaneous and open to possibilities as you learn to live with fewer assumptions and labels about yourself and others

- Aware of your emotional responses and your mental activity and habits

- Sensitive to your body and its signals of stress and relaxation

- Kind to yourself as you discover who you are and what you want, and you learn to say what you mean

- Intuitive, listening to your own wisdom and making more nourishing choices

- Compassionate to others and present with loving attention

- Soul-centered as you shift your center point from the external world to your own loving, beautiful, wise essence

With the confidence that comes from leading-edge science, along with timeless meditation practices and awareness exercises, the 8-week program will serve as a guide along your journey of continuous, lifelong transformation.

The Five Essentials of Meditation

Before you begin your journey to becoming soul-centered, there are five basic keys to success in meditation that I want to address. These are: (1) it's okay to have thoughts during meditation, (2) don't try too hard, (3) let go of expectations, (4) be kind to yourself, and (5) stick with it. And it's important to know this: *The way you meditate and treat yourself in meditation is the way you treat yourself as you live your life.*

1. It's Okay to Have Thoughts

If you're thinking, *I probably can't do this program because I have too many thoughts,* then you are not alone. Perhaps you've already tried to meditate for a few minutes once or twice, and it "didn't work." You sat down, closed your eyes, and tried to clear your mind but couldn't. Then you gave up.

Students in my classes often tell me, "I can't stop thinking." My reply is, "That's right, *you* can't stop the thoughts." I explain that you can't stop thoughts by thinking about *not thinking,* because the nature of the mind is *to think,* like the nature of your eyes is *to see.* If you try to stop thinking, your effort will make you frustrated and possibly give you a headache.

You don't need to completely stop thinking during meditation. Instead, the meditation practices you will learn in this program naturally settle your mind and body, making it easier to experience the quieter levels of your thoughts and impulses. Sometimes the thought process even stops for a moment or two; before another thought or sensation arises, you'll have experienced the silence that is always present, underlying the thoughts, the silence of your soul. This stillness of mind is not *created* by you stopping your thoughts. Instead, it is a natural process that is always available to be experienced—it is merely *revealed* through meditating.

2. Don't Try Too Hard

I once taught meditation to a heart surgeon and his wife on New Year's Day (he had called and set up an appointment at 9 A.M., wanting to start the year off right). After they learned to meditate he asked how he could "get good at it." I responded by asking him how he got to be "good" at surgery. *Practice, right?* Well, it's the same with meditation.

At first, you may try to do it "right." But you soon find that overly working at it, trying too hard, forcing it, or concentrating only creates more thoughts and bad habits. You can't *try* to do anything without the mind getting involved. Instead of expending mental effort or trying to have a certain experience, you'll learn to refocus your attention, gently. Contrary to what so many believe, you don't get good at meditation by trying hard to do it. Instead, the practice requires ease and effortlessness.

With meditation, your mind and body will settle down naturally, and as with any natural process, too much effort can ruin the process. For example, trying to go to sleep, even if you're tired, can make you miserable. Trying to come up with a new idea and force through a creative block is the same way—it rarely works. Trying to meditate is similar, because meditation is an effortless pursuit. The only effort you put in is the effort to set aside the time and space for your regular practice. Some of us are in the habit of having to be doing something in order to feel a sense of satisfaction, and that includes "doing" meditation by trying hard at it. Instead, meditation trains you to get comfortable "being," just being yourself without effort.

3. Let Go of Expectations

You may have preconceived notions of what is supposed to be going on during meditation and how you should feel or what you should experience. Many of us have seen pictures of monks in robes or yogis sitting cross-legged, and some have heard stories about the wild experiences some meditators have, but I love to teach those who have no expectations about meditation. First timers come and sit with me for 15 to 20 minutes, then report that they felt great and that it was easy. I attribute this to "beginner's mind," an attitude you'll learn more about in Week Three.

During meditation, you'll have all kinds of experiences—some you'll like better than others, and some you'll want to repeat in your next meditation. It's important to treat each meditation as innocently as the first time you learned, and expect nothing. Let go of expectations or wanting your meditation to go a certain way. The body and mind are intelligent and will naturally do what they need to do to eliminate stress and to create a nourishing effect.

I'm often asked, "How will I know if I'm doing it right?" My answer is that when you approach meditation without expectations, without trying "too hard" or attempting to control your experience, and with a sense of ease and welcome for whatever experiences arise, then you are *doing it right.* Instead of judging your practice as good or bad based on the experiences you have in meditation, see if it's working another way: Notice whether you are happier, more relaxed, less stressed, more creative, more perceptive, and more appreciative of your life.

4. Be Kind to Yourself

An essential key to meditating correctly is to *be kind to yourself.* This is one of the most important things I have learned through my years of practicing and teaching meditation. While it should go without saying, I continue to say it because many people have learned to be tough on themselves. Being tough on yourself does not help change your behavior; it's simply a bad habit. Don't get down on yourself in meditation if your mind wanders, or you get bored, or the experiences you have don't fulfill your expectations. Instead, be gentle toward yourself as you commit to transforming your life. Be nice to yourself when you're not meditating, too. Don't compare your experience to others' experiences. All is well.

5. Stick with It

Finally, meditation only works if you *stick with it* and don't give up. During your meditation period your mind may wander, you may feel restless, you have a brilliant idea you must write down, or you think of something else you simply must do (like check your e-mail); and you may want to give up. But don't. Simply begin again and return your awareness to the focus of your meditation. Have the discipline to do the practices and stick with the entire meditation period you committed to each day, whether it's five minutes or half an hour, even if you're antsy or bored.

By staying with the practice, you will create a new relationship with your mind. As you let the thoughts and impulses come and go without taking action, you become less reactive to a thought and instead become the witness to your mental activity. This will lead you to a deeper understanding of how your mind works. Often when you feel fidgety or frustrated in meditation, it's an indication that you're releasing a lot of stress. If you stick with the practice, the stress will soon dissipate and you'll experience a "meditator's high." Don't quit before the bliss! Don't quit the program; stay with it for eight weeks. Meditating every day will give you the benefits, but *not meditating* won't. Even if you don't think anything is happening in meditation, science shows dramatic changes in the brains and bodies of consistent meditators. And you'll soon believe it once you see the benefits.

How to Use this Program

This program is a course of eight lessons. I suggest that after reading straight through the book, you go back and read one lesson each week. Read and reread it as you see fit, and thoroughly absorb it. Then, as outlined in the table at the end of each lesson, practice the meditations and the awareness exercises.

The best thing about this program is that you can start right now without changing a thing about yourself—not your diet, your religion, your outfit, your beliefs—*nothing*. All that's required is the willingness to begin and setting aside a short time every day for practice. (You may want to consult with your doctor before beginning this regimen, especially if you have health challenges.) And for all you busy people who think you can't meditate because you don't have time, I've seen changes in people who meditate for only five minutes, once a day. Of course, twice a day is better, and about 30 minutes a day is a sure bet for changing the hardwiring of your brain and transforming your life.

○ ○

Now is a good time to ask yourself: *What is my intention? How do I want to live my life? How do I want my life to transform?* If you don't discover the answers right away, be patient. Eventually the answers will come. Each meditation you engage in will reveal, or be inherently inspired by, your sincere intention.

Let's get started!

○ ○ ○

WEEK ONE

AWARENESS: BE HERE NOW

"The past is gone, the future is not yet here. If we do not go back to ourselves in the present moment, we cannot be in touch with life."

— THICH NHAT HANH, VIETNAMESE ZEN TEACHER

Welcome to the first week of your 8-week program. This week I will introduce you to two awareness exercises: *Breath Awareness* and *Body Awareness*. These exercises will help you become familiar with two elements essential to any meditation you engage in: (1) paying attention with nonjudgmental, gentle awareness, and (2) giving that attention a particular focus—usually something you think, hear, see, or feel.

Throughout this program, you will learn to focus your attention with what is best described as an "easy awareness." To get a sense of it right now, bring your awareness to your right hand, and just feel it for a moment. Now, focus your attention on your left, and feel it. It was probably easy and effortless to shift your focus from right to left. As you progress throughout the 8-week program, you'll use that same easy awareness and that effortless shifting of attention in meditation, whether you are focusing on your breath, your body, a sensation, an image, an activity, a sound, an idea, or a thing.

1

This week's *Breath Awareness* and *Body Awareness* exercises are designed to train your attention in three ways: (1) attending to the present moment, (2) easily turning your attention inward to your inner realm, and (3) focusing clearly on one thing at a time. You also learn *Mindful Living Exercises* to enliven your present-moment awareness throughout the day. This training will help you with the formal sitting meditation practice you will learn next week.

Many people who come to me to learn to meditate complain that their life has become unfulfilling. It seems to be composed of a series of rote activities, like going to work, taking care of the kids, and household chores. They repeat the same behaviors day in and day out, checking things off their to-do list, while focusing on the next thing rather than attending to what is happening in each moment. They are on autopilot; and this can make life seem un-interesting, and uninspiring. It also keeps them from being aware of how they're feeling or what their choices are. They forget what inspires them and how joyful life can be.

Whether you're reading a book, listening to a friend, eating a piece of fruit, going for a walk, or driving your kids to soccer, your life is made up of one moment following another. When you live your life with your awareness engaged in the present moment and learn to *be here now,* you appreciate the simplest things, and ordinary tasks begin to have new dimensions and depth. You begin to slow down, and stop rushing around so much. You become more self-aware and connected to what you're feeling, thinking, and doing. You notice habitual patterns that have kept you stuck; and as you notice them, they begin to dissipate. You discover the possibilities in each moment and make better choices, access your creativity and feel more inspired, and experience the freedom and peace that are ever present. The meditation practices and mindfulness exercises you learn this week will bring you these benefits.

Mindfulness: Living in the Now

One evening I was talking with my friend Joyce from Texas about getting the most out of life. "We've all heard the kingdom of

God is within us," she said, "but I realized recently that the kingdom of God is *now.*" I love that idea. *Now!* Now is so inclusive—everybody has access to *now,* regardless of their age, race, financial status, education, religious beliefs, or intelligence. This moment, right now, is when we live our life. And anyone, anywhere, can experience it.

Life does not take place in the past or in the future; it is happening right now. This very moment is when your life is lived. All your thoughts, feelings, and sensations are experienced in the present moment. The present moment is when you make choices, set intentions, make plans, take action, access your intuition, get inspired, feel your feelings, and even fall in love. You breathe in the present moment. Your body exists in this moment. Memories of the past and ideas about the future pale in comparison to the reality of the life you're living *now.* Being here, now, with your full awareness, is essential for living a soul-centered life.

Mindfulness is when you are engaged in and fully attentive to what you are doing and experiencing in each and every moment, while also being aware of your emotions, thoughts, and judgments. Mindfulness can be practiced anytime, whether you are sitting quietly for a meditation session, reading this page, or going for a walk in nature. You can practice mindfulness by giving your full attention to any routine activity, such as taking a shower or brushing your teeth. Mindfulness, along with meditation and other present-moment-awareness practices, trains your awareness to be in the now.

You can easily refocus your awareness to the now by tuning in to your senses, paying attention to your breath, or focusing on how your body feels. Let's give it a try:

> Give yourself a moment to bring your attention to the way your body feels as you sit. Relax your shoulders and belly. Feel where your body meets the chair, where your feet meet the floor. Notice how your body is supported and aligned. Notice if a story about your body arises; if it does, shift your focus from thoughts *about* your body to the sensations *of* your body, feeling from the inside out.

Next, welcome the sounds surrounding you at this moment. Let them meet your awareness. Simply listen, and when you begin to tell a story about the sounds (where they're coming from, who's making them, and so on), gently return your attention to the experience of listening, paying attention to the actual sounds as they arise and change.

Finally, shift your attention to your breathing. Feel the air as it moves in and out of your body. You don't have to change a thing or regulate your breath. Simply become aware of the in-and-out movement of the air through your nostrils. Do this for a few breaths.

There, you've done it—you've anchored your awareness in the present moment! This and every moment is an opportunity to be mindful and fully experience life by focusing on the simplest of activities—feeling and breathing. Later in this book we'll address self-awareness, including the awareness of what you're thinking and your emotional state, but for now, let's keep it simple so you can commit to this easy practice.

You breathe in the present moment. Your body exists in the present moment. By bringing your focus to how your body and breath feel, you train your awareness to focus on the moment at hand. Your life is happening right now. Tomorrow, or the next moment, will arrive and be experienced in the present moment, too. *Now* is the time of your life. *Right now.*

Your Wandering Mind

Each of us has about 1,000 thoughts per hour, with the average person thinking 12,000 thoughts per day (some folks even get up to 50,000 thoughts daily), according to a National Science Foundation report. You are not aware of all those thoughts, because half the time that you're "thinking," your brain is actually on autopilot. Instead of *you* directing the thoughts, your mind is following a program that keeps it focused on a myriad of concerns, quandaries, and dilemmas. Operating on autopilot shuts you off from your feelings, inspiration, and the direct experience of your own life.

The tendency of the mind to wander is the result both of early training and of basic physiological wiring. A 2010 Harvard University research study shows that not only do people spend almost half the time thinking about something other than what they're doing, but that when the mind wanders this way, it leaves the person unhappy. On the other hand, research subjects reported they were happiest when they were completely focused on an activity, whether it was exercising, making love, or engaging in conversation.

When the mind wanders, it's often focused on a time other than the present, a habit that starts when we are very young and continues throughout life. Children are trained to dutifully reflect on the past and look ahead into the future. Five-year-old Shelby doesn't want to wait for her birthday party on the weekend to have that cake, she wants it *right now*. And *no*, she doesn't remember what she learned in school today; she doesn't want to talk about the past, it's *boring*. Seven-year-old Justin has no idea what he wants to be when he grows up—never gave it a thought. But we encourage them to think about the past and the future, over and over. And so the habits begin.

As adults, some of us develop a tendency to focus attention in the past, wishing we could either change it or go back to live in it, nostalgic for "the good old days." Others find that they focus on the future, how life will be better "someday" when they finally get to live out their dreams—or they get the job, spouse, car, or house they've wanted. With a focus on a time other than now, the present moment is reduced to a time when nothing of significance can be accomplished. For example, when you plan a big event such as a wedding or a vacation, you spend hours thinking about what will happen. The present moment takes a backseat to the *idea* of the big day, as your mind plans the details.

Present-moment awareness doesn't mean that you have to stop planning or that you must abandon all plans for your future.

It doesn't have anything to do with settling for less, giving up, forgetting about the past, or pretending future responsibilities don't exist. However, the reality is that you can't make choices or take any kind of action in the past or in the future, because choices and actions can only occur in the present. So that's where we should have most of our focus. Everything you have to deal with in real life, as opposed to your mind's projections of future and past, is handled in the present moment. The present moment is the only time you can access creativity, make choices, take action, set intentions, reminisce, and make plans.

If you have a big project or an event coming up that you need to plan, I suggest you set aside a specific time during your day to get completely involved in planning it. Make an appointment. When you notice your mind drifting off to plan the future or dream about the past randomly throughout the day, say to yourself, *I'll think about that later*. Then, at the appointed time, do just that: set your intentions, sketch out your plan, or dream about your life. Having an appointed planning time really helps to calm the mind.

We all want to be happy, and focusing on the present moment cultivates happiness. Just as your mind got into the habit of going on autopilot or wandering into the future or past, it can be trained to stay focused in the now. When you're focused on the present moment, life is more vivid—colors are brighter, sounds are more beautiful, you notice the true sensations of your body and what food actually tastes like. You are more attentive to yourself, your friends, your family, and your surroundings. Life takes on a magical quality. You feel inspired, playful, spontaneous, relaxed, and happy. You stop to smell the roses, because you notice them. With awareness training, you can truly experience how beautiful life can be.

Chopping and Planning

As a program director at The Chopra Center, I spent each day at my desk, coordinating mind-body health programs and educational events. I had a calendar of programs planned for a year out. Sometimes I would attend a program I'd set up months before and find it difficult to enjoy myself. Although I'd been meditating at that point for six years and was very present while in meditation, *outside* of meditation my mind would just skip to planning the next task I had to do.

This was a habit of mine. Even though I had lived a life rich with varied experiences, I hadn't really savored them—I hadn't been truly *there* for them. Of course, I had the occasional moments of being totally present in the face of great beauty, or in a moment of expanded awareness, or while immersed in nature, but it wasn't how I normally attended to my life.

I decided to go and spend some time in India. There, I lived and meditated for up to five hours a day in a traditional ashram in Kerala. I was assigned to work in the kitchen, helping make fruit salad for breakfast for hundreds of people every day. I peeled and cut fruit as the sun rose, listening to the other residents chanting in the meditation hall as they did each morning. I silently repeated the chants while I worked. When I became aware that my mind was engaged in some other place and time, I refocused. The chopping and the chanting were in the present moment, so by simply refocusing on the action and the sound, I became more grounded in present-moment awareness.

When I returned to the States, I struck out on my next adventure and became a resident in a Southern California meditation community, a Zen Buddhist monastic training center where I had previously attended a few weekend retreats. During my two years of living at the Zen Mountain Center, I was immersed in Buddhist philosophy and meditated extensively. The meditations, rituals, and practices adhered to the traditions of a formal Zen monastery. I was given the name *Yuko*, which means "mysterious illumination." It suited me because I love a good mystery.

As it was in India, my work practice in the Zen Center was often in the kitchen. It was the perfect place to continue the practice of being present while in activity: chopping vegetables, doing dishes, making bread, stirring, sautéing, and steaming. While they didn't use the same term for it, my life there was one long continuous *mindfulness* practice. Practice for sure, because once again, to my dismay, I'd be chopping and chopping while planning and planning. I would plan how I could be at the Zen Center forever, how I could meditate more, and how I could be happier. It was frustrating to fall back into this habit of mind, but I kept bringing my attention back to the moment. Eventually, I was able to fully and completely focus my attention for longer periods on what I was doing, one thing at a time. These moments were completely engaging and satisfying.

Then I was promoted to *tenzo,* the head cook. With my increased responsibilities, my mental wandering and planning began *again*. My mind was filled with schedules and measurements, shopping lists and menus. I had the desire to be present in each moment, but I also felt the responsibility to organize at the same time. However, once I realized that I had to plan a time for planning, I was able to stop my wandering mind from interrupting my present-moment awareness. My job became a sweet experience.

Mindfulness and Multitasking

How do you know when you're not attending to the present moment? Long periods of time might go by before *you* notice, but perhaps others notice right away. Do people (such as your spouse) tell you that you're not listening to what they're saying? Do you sometimes read an e-mail from a friend or co-worker and a minute later have no recollection of what you read when someone asks you about it? What about sitting down to a delicious meal and suddenly seeing that the food is gone, but not remembering eating? You may call this disappearance of your attention "spacing out"; I call it "mindlessness." And mindlessness causes stress.

While your brain and body have evolved naturally to multitask, the "get it done" culture we live in now requires greater and greater degrees of multitasking. Everyone expects it both at home and at work, and we're all used to it. When you're doing one thing and focused on something else, your attention is split. As you talk on the phone, you can empty the dishwasher or scan your e-mail. You drive along to an appointment while eating lunch, or watch TV while exercising at the gym. So what's the problem? The result is that your focus is half here and half there, but never fully anywhere. In pursuit of doing more and splitting your attention, you miss important moments in your life.

Splitting your attention also creates stress. The constant effort required to multitask puts far more demand on your brain than does doing one thing at a time, according to researchers from Massachusetts Institute of Technology (MIT), who found that we can only focus on one or two items at a time. When forced to concentrate on doing different tasks at the same time, the brain's limited processing capacity gets overloaded, resulting in less clear thinking and the slowing down of mental processes. Another study shows that being distracted during an activity can also create stress. Participants who were interrupted by incoming e-mail while working on a task reported higher levels of stress after just 20 minutes. They felt that their workloads were greater and required more mental effort to complete than those who weren't interrupted.

Split attention and distractions can create stress and lower the quality of your life, but meditation can help. In one study, people had to deal with simultaneous instant messages, alarms, phone calls, texts, and in-person questions in a 20-minute exercise. After, those taught to meditate were far less stressed than those who weren't. The meditators performed the tasks while paying attention to their breath and telling themselves to slow down. This helped them stay present to and focused on their immediate experience rather than their evaluation of it. They felt more in control and less fearful, realizing that they didn't have to respond to immediate demands on their attention. They learned how to focus without stress.

One key to being less stressed and more present is to just do whatever you're doing more slowly. Slow down on purpose. You can do this while driving, walking, reading, eating, drinking, or anytime. You might find at first that slowing down drives you a bit crazy, especially if your habit is to rush through your tasks. But when you find yourself in a hurry, ask yourself, *What is all the rush about?* You might find you're simply being mind*less* when you could be mind*ful.*

Cultivating Self-Awareness

Throughout this 8-week program, you are encouraged to feel all of your feelings as they come up, whether they're physical sensations or emotional responses, and whether or not you "like" them. This is a holistic approach to life—leaving nothing out. Only when you become aware of your thoughts and emotions and feel them—instead of repressing or being taken over by them— can you develop a new relationship to them.

You learn that thoughts and emotions are not "who you are"; they are not your inner essence. Once you realize this, you are less controlled by stimuli or sensations. You cultivate a *responsive* rather than *reactive* relationship with your thoughts, feelings, and sensations. You can thoughtfully choose what to do, say, or think next. You notice what feels right because you're paying attention, and this makes it easier to take action and make more nourishing choices.

When your awareness is in the present, you experience life in a different way—you feel more connected to everything. Some of my students tell me that when they became more aware of the present moment, they felt more loving, peaceful, and fulfilled, independent of their life's circumstance. You too can access this ever-present inner peace and contentment. If you find yourself saying, *Peace? That's impossible. I have so many problems to deal with*, ask yourself what "problems" you have right this moment—not yesterday, tomorrow, next year, or even five minutes from now. What is wrong in *this moment*, really? You might find out some of the problems you face are *not here, not now*—but rather exist only in your thoughts about what might happen or did happen.

Here is what I learned: When you're feeling anxious or fearful, it's a clue that your focus is likely in the future; when you're feeling grief or depression, your attention is probably in the past. If you're feeling angry or critical, your focus is outside of yourself; and if you're feeling ashamed or embarrassed, you are probably tuned in to an unclear or distorted image of yourself. Your emotions are clues to *where* your attention is focused. So your job is to notice and allow yourself to feel how you feel; then return your attention, sweetly, right back to where you are and what you're doing now. It's more peaceful here.

Being Present with the Unpleasant

When life is stressful or traumatic or you are suffering in some way, it may seem easier to focus your attention anywhere but on the painful situation at hand. So you distract yourself. Distractions can include focusing on the future, working too hard, running away (mentally or physically), compulsively eating or exercising, indulging in alcohol or drugs, spacing out, or scattering your attention from one thing to the next. It's natural to want to avoid feeling sensations you deem unpleasant or difficult, but whether you like it or not, whether you plan for them or not, they do come up. Just as the good ones do.

Some people, especially if they experience a tragedy or heartache, believe that if they start crying they'll never stop. They might feel that the pain would "kill" them. Either way, they believe that if they truly feel their emotions, they will lose control and something bad will happen. Fortunately, meditation can help you develop a sense of safety, so that when a challenging emotion or a painful physical sensation arises, you feel centered enough to experience it. You allow yourself to feel the sensations in your body and learn by experience that pain is not permanent. Pain always has a beginning, middle, and end, even if it initially doesn't seem that way.

When painful physical sensations arise and you don't fully allow yourself to experience them, it can cause stress. As you become more present to the moment through body awareness or meditation, you become more fluent in the language of your own body, and you begin to gently feel everything and bear witness to what arises—even uncomfortable thoughts, emotions, and sensations. When you feel pain, fear, or anger, practice locating and feeling the sensations in your body without resisting them, bracing against them, or trying to change them. Experience them— you don't have to act on them. When you fully experience what is going on inside, your attention has an effect on the sensations that arise, and you will notice that they eventually shift or come to a natural end. The practice of meditation is the best way to gently dissolve the residue of past trauma and physical pains we all carry with us.

One of the most challenging times to focus on the present moment is when you are ill or receive a serious diagnosis. Yet this is the time when such awareness is the most valuable.

This reminds me of one of my meditation students who sent me a newspaper article about her friend, a 51-year-old woman with cancer. This friend was a type A personality who knew success in everything she did, including running and completing several long-distance marathons. My student sent this note along with the article:

> *My friend just found out she has a life-threatening, rare cancer—only about 300 people a year are diagnosed with it. She has to have a special treatment out of state that her insurance company won't pay for. She's focusing on appealing her insurance company's decision and getting the money together for the specialized surgery, which she will follow with radiation treatments. Do you have any advice for her?*

I did. It was the same advice I'd been offering for years. I wrote:

In addition to getting the surgery and the radiation, I recommend that your friend learn to meditate and practice it at least once a day, every day, now and after the surgery. Meditation will help alleviate the stress she faces—mentally, emotionally, and physically. Stress has been shown to suppress the immune system, and when the immune system is compromised, it can't fight off the cancer cells as efficiently. Stress can also inhibit the body's natural healing process once the surgery and treatments are over.

While all of this vying for insurance coverage is going on and while waiting for her surgery and treatments, I encourage your friend to bring her attention back to the present moment. The tendency for most of us is to focus on the future, to say, "When my cancer is gone, then I'll get on with my life," but this way of thinking can keep her from experiencing the life she is living now. Of course, she needs to spend time planning and thinking about the future—to round up funds, look for answers, take care of her family's future needs. But does she give herself time to slow down and enjoy the life she already has? Does she give herself permission to feel all her feelings? Experience the world she lives in now? I suggest she enjoy each day: leisurely meals, mindful walks, time in nature, and the company of family and good friends. Those little things create a precious life, whether you have cancer or not. This moment, this very moment, is all we can be sure of.

I gave my student some simple mindfulness anchors to pass on to her friend, such as paying attention to the body and the breath. (You'll learn these exercises at the end of this lesson.) These practices would help her, even if the cancer didn't go away.

It's important to be present for our lives, whether we are healthy or not, happy with our job or not, in love or not, feeling good about ourselves or not . . . because we never know what is going to happen next. And being present is the best way to be prepared for anything.

A Meditator's Story: Childlike Awareness

Shortly after her first son was born, Jeanna came to see me. A busy public-relations professional with a thriving business in Phoenix, she'd diagnosed herself with postpartum depression and mild anxiety. Now she was looking for a way to enjoy her new motherhood and life in general.

"I find it hard to be present for my life," she told me when we first met. "I have this amazing son, but I can barely sit still long enough to enjoy him. I'm constantly cooking, cleaning, or doing laundry. I feel more like a human *doing* than a human *being*."

Jeanna had a difficult time being present in the moment with another—especially a demanding newborn. In fact, most of her life had been spent focusing on the future. She told me that even as a young child, while at an amusement park or at the beach, she'd ask her parents what they were going to do the next day. Now as an adult, that habitual focus on a time outside of the present moment was causing Jeanna stress, and she found herself unable to engage in the moments with her son.

"It's a strange predicament to describe," she said. "I have this feeling that there's somewhere else I should be or something else I should be doing, other than what I *am* doing. It's like I'm running from myself, and it's completely crazy from an outside perspective, I'm sure. I have a wonderful husband, a dear child, a great house, and an exciting job. Most people would be grateful for my life, and here I am looking for something more—and I don't even know what that is."

I suggested that Jeanna take one of my beginner meditation classes and practice mindfulness while in her daily life, training her attention to be in the present moment whenever she could. The meditation would help her eliminate some of the stress, and the mindfulness practices would allow her to have some peaceful moments in her day. I also suggested that whenever she was with her son, she follow his lead. "Take your cues from him—he can be a great teacher," I advised. "Pay attention to how he pays attention. Watch what he's focusing on and keep bringing your attention back to that. Let him show you how to stay present and focused on one thing at a time."

Jeanna learned to meditate and started to practice mindfulness. When I heard from her again, she had some good news to report. "Thank you, thank you!" she said. "You were right—my son is my best teacher! He's just starting to walk, and I make it my practice to follow him around. I sit still when he does, move when he does, and pay attention to what he is paying attention to. He loves having Mommy playing with him more, and I'm so much more present with him and generally calmer. My new meditation practice has centered me and allowed me to focus on what or who is right in front of me. It's a fabulous feeling to know I can find meaning and purpose in the simple moments of my life."

Practices and Exercises to Cultivate Awareness

Mindful Living Exercises

As you go about your everyday routine, you can engage your awareness and your senses, making any activity a mindful one. Choose any task, such as taking a shower, brushing your teeth, doing the dishes, or washing your hands. You can start by simply choosing to do the activity more slowly. Here are some examples of exercises you can use anytime throughout the day to train your present-moment awareness:

— *When you wash your hands,* feel the way your body aligns as you stand or bend over the sink. Feel the water as it meets your hands. Notice the temperature of the water and the sensations as your hands go from dry to wet. Listen to the sounds of the water. Smell the scent of the soap and feel its texture. Observe the way your hands move. Feel how your wet hands dry, or the texture of the towel.

— *When you drink water,* pick up the glass or bottle and notice the way the light reflects on both it and the liquid inside. Notice how it feels as you hold it. Notice the weight and the temperature. Feel the sensations as you lift the water to your mouth and sip and swallow. Feel the water traveling through your body.

— *Each time the phone rings,* pause for a moment before you pick it up. In this moment, you can make a choice: answer the call, let it go to voice mail, or let it ring one more time while you allow yourself a deep breath. You can also use the ring as a reminder to bring your awareness to your body and scan it for signs of comfort or discomfort. It's good to know that you have a choice, and by interrupting the habitual reaction of immediately answering the phone, you become more aware of the choices available in *every* moment.

— *After you get into your car,* give yourself a minute in silence before you start the engine. Close your eyes and simply sit. With your eyes closed, you'll notice that your other senses are more active. Feel your body, feel the flow of your breath. Feel the temperature of the seat, the air. Then, when you are settled and ready, start your car. Notice the sounds. Feel the movement and vibration of the vehicle. Feel the sensations in your body as you drive. Take it easy and slow down, just a little. Don't tailgate or try to make it through the yellow lights. At the red lights and stop signs, give yourself a moment to relax your body and tune in to your breath. Smile to yourself and make the journey as important as the destination.

— *When you find yourself waiting,* it's a perfect time to practice present-moment awareness. Whether you're in a waiting room, grabbing lunch with a friend, or in a line at the grocery store, bring your attention to the moment at hand. Notice the people around you and your physical surroundings. What do you sense as you stand there? How do you feel?

Recently, I was heading to a meditation retreat. My plane arrived late, as did my shuttle, and it looked like I was going to miss dinner at the retreat center. I asked the shuttle driver to take me to a grocery store. I ran in and grabbed a snack, then got in the long checkout line. I was impatient to get to the retreat center. I wanted the moment to be over fast—I wanted to get in and get out—and was focused solely on my future satisfaction. Suddenly, as I was standing in line I remembered something that the Zen teacher Thich Nhat Hanh says: "I've arrived. This is it." I instantly realized that this moment in line was the moment I was living my life. I brought my attention back to the way my body felt standing there; I felt the sensations of my breath, I shifted my attention, and I fully arrived at the moment at hand, holding my snack, waiting in line with these sweet people I hadn't even noticed before.

Choose any of these or other ordinary activities to remind you to be aware of what you're doing as you do it. I have a mindfulness bell on my computer that goes off at random intervals to remind me to arrive in the present moment. When it chimes, I stop what I'm doing and either close my eyes for a moment or look out the window. I turn my attention to my breath and how my body feels. I take a deep breath, relax, and sit up straight. You can do this, too.

Breath Awareness

Paying attention to the breath is another simple way to connect to the present moment and become more self-aware. This is a relaxing, easy practice anyone can do, anywhere, anytime. It's a great preparation for the sitting meditation you will learn next week.

Read through the following instructions. Review them again each day before you practice. It's natural not to remember each and every step, but as time goes by it will become second nature. Remember to let go of expectations, be kind to yourself, and complete your entire practice period. Practice *Breath Awareness* for 10 minutes the first time, and 15 minutes each day thereafter this first week. Here's how:

— Determine how long you'll be doing this practice before you start. Keep track of the time by looking at a clock or watch. Don't set an alarm that will make you get up to shut it off.

— You can sit or lie down for this exercise. Your eyes can be open, half-closed, or closed. Turn off music, sounds, TVs, or what have you.

— Begin by breathing naturally through your nose.

— Bring your awareness to each breath, focusing on the movement and sensations the air creates as it moves in and out of your body.

— As the breath enters and leaves through your nostrils, notice the cool air on the inhale, the warmer air on the exhale.

— Feel your chest and back rise and fall on the inhalation and exhalation.

— Feel your belly expand and contract.

— This practice isn't about imagining or controlling the breath, but simply feeling its sensations. Allow the breath to come and go in its own natural pattern. There's nothing to figure out. Nothing to control. Nothing to change.

— Keep your focus on each breath. Then, for a few breaths, let your attention rest on the natural pause between the exhale and inhale.

— Whenever you notice that your attention has drifted away from your breath—shifting to a noise, a thought, or some other distraction—simply refocus your attention to the breath.

— This is a practice, so don't give yourself a hard time about losing focus. Distractions are natural. Be kind to yourself without concern for how many times you drift off. Don't judge your experience based on how many times your attention drifts away.

— If you get distracted by physical sensations, recognize them but don't attempt to figure out why they're happening, or go into a story about them. Simply keep the sensations company with your awareness, exploring the sensations and feelings until they dissipate. When they do, gently return your attention to your breath.

— You may find your breathing spontaneously gets faster or slower, deeper or shallower; it may even pause for a moment. Observe any changes without controlling, resisting, anticipating, or expecting anything. Do nothing but observe.

— Rest your attention on the breath and its sensations for your predetermined period of time. When the period comes to an end, take your attention off your breath. Sit or lie still for a few minutes. After a few minutes, slowly open your eyes (if they were closed), and take your time moving back into activity.

Body Awareness

Like the *Breath Awareness* exercise, this exercise will help you be more intimate with how you feel, which leads to more self-awareness. Adopt the attitude of an explorer as you do this exercise; feel, watch, listen, and detect sensations as they come and go. As you explore, you become the witness of your body and breath and this helps you develop present-moment awareness. I suggest you do this exercise for 15 minutes each afternoon or evening this week. Here's how:

— Do this practice with your eyes open, half-closed, or closed.

— Sit up comfortably.

— Let your breath remain natural, breathing through your nose. It might slow down, speed up, get deeper or shallower, or stop for a moment. Feel it, and let it be as it is.

— Move your awareness slowly, deliberately, from your head to your toes, in a continuous flow. You'll be doing this a few times. The first time that you scan your body, you will relax each area.

— Feel your body from the inside out, noticing every sensation, relaxing each area and any tension you find. Allow your attention to rest for a few seconds or so on each body part in a continuous fashion. Bring your awareness to your:

- Head (including your scalp, forehead, ears, eyes, nose, cheeks, mouth, tongue, chin, and jaw)
- Neck
- Shoulders
- Each arm, elbow, and wrist
- Each hand and each finger
- Chest and diaphragm
- Belly
- Upper, mid, and lower back
- Hips, pelvis, rear
- Each thigh, knee, and calf
- Each foot and each toe

— Once complete, scan your body a second time from head to toes. This time, let your attention rest on areas of your body where you find pain, discomfort, or illness.

— Allow yourself to "be with" any sensations, even discomfort, rather than trying to make the sensations go away, change them, or create a story about what's going on there. You may be used to avoiding certain areas. This exercise is an opportunity to allow yourself to experience whatever sensation is actually present with curiosity and nonjudgmental awareness.

— As you experience sensations in your body, you may find you begin to tell yourself a story about a specific area such as, *My knees hurt from a skiing accident; My stomach is too big, I should exercise more;* or *I am too tired to do this, I didn't get enough sleep.* Once you realize that you're storytelling, gently return your attention to the area you are focused on.

— Be patient and kind to yourself. Simply feel the sensations of that area from the inside out; do not focus on the thought about it. Being present with the pain or discomfort without trying to change it is called "bearing witness." Be with each area until you know it's time to move to the next.

— Don't judge your experience or worry about how many times your attention drifts away from the body.

— Welcome whatever you feel. If you don't have any distinct sensations, welcome that, too. When thoughts about the future or past distract you from your focus, notice them, then simply return your focus to your body's sensations.

— Continue this practice for the predetermined period of time. When you're finished, take your attention off your body. Notice your state of mind as you sit still for another few minutes.

— After a few minutes, slowly open your eyes (if they were closed), and take your time moving back into activity.

Schedule of Practices

Week One: Suggested Daily Practices	
AM	Breath Awareness: 15 Minutes
PM	Body Awareness: 15 Minutes

Additional Awareness Exercises	
Anytime	Slow down
	Mindful Living Exercises

Insights for Success

This first week, it's best to do the exercises for a total of 30 minutes each day. You can practice them once or twice a day with the recommended times being early morning before your day gets going, and in the evening between work and dinner. You can practice any time of day that suits your temperament, but ideally choose a time when your heart is at a resting rate and your stomach isn't too full. Your body likes rhythm and regularity, so keep that in mind. Set yourself up to succeed. Once you choose a time, put it in your schedule, just as you would an important meeting.

Remember, this program trains your brain and transforms your life. It only works if you *do* it, not if you're just reading each chapter, even if you recognize the truth of what you're reading. You must do the practices each week. If you would like to be guided in this week's awareness practices, you can go online to **www .McLeanMeditation.com/guidedmeditations** where I've recorded some of these practices on audio and video to help you.

If you find you're easily charmed by your thoughts or by what's going on around you as you do the practices and exercises, remember that this is normal. Eventually, with practice, they won't hook you or disturb you. There is no shortcut for this. All meditators have to learn to create a new relationship with distractions and thoughts.

The exercises for this week will begin to shift your attention from the *idea* of your life to the actual *experience* of your life. You are training your attention so you can be truly present and fully attentive to what you're doing and feeling rather than projecting into the future or thinking about what has happened. Some of my students have told me that their life has become one long mindfulness practice as they move from the domain of "doing" to "being" while in activity.

As you go through the program and learn new practices, some will resonate with you more than others. I suggest you practice each a few times, but if you find yourself enjoying one more than another, then do that one more often. This week's mindfulness practices are the keystones for self-awareness and focusing on the moment at hand, and they prepare you for the sitting meditation you'll learn in Week Two.

○ ○ ○

PEACE: STRESS LESS

"Sometimes the most important thing in a whole day is the rest we take between two deep breaths."

— FROM THE DIARIES OF ETTY HILLESUM,
DIED IN AUSCHWITZ 1943

In Week One's mindfulness practices, you cultivated more awareness: awareness of the present moment and awareness of yourself. You may have noticed as you practiced the awareness exercises that it was easier to focus some days than it was on other days, and that it was more difficult to keep your attention focused whenever you felt stressed-out. That is often the case, and it's natural.

This week, we take a good look at stress, including its causes and how to recognize its effects in your mind and body. You'll learn how to get back to your center quickly in stressful moments with *Peacefinder Exercises* and *Long, Slow, Deep Breathing*. You'll also learn to relieve stress in your mind and body through the classic practice I introduce this week, a *Sitting Meditation*.

We were not born stressed-out. It's something that happens to many of us over time. In fact, to an infant, the world is a wondrous, friendly place. It's a place full of possibilities and fun! You once felt like that, too. As a child, you were loving and present. You sensed that whatever was going on around you was *for* you.

But as you got older, tension accumulated in your nervous system, and your perception of this once-friendly world changed. It became less than friendly. Life started to happen *to* you rather than *for* you. Instead of welcoming life—and all the people and events in it—you began to just *deal with* what's going on. Stress is what causes that shift, and it's often so gradual and so subtle, you may not have even noticed that it has happened. I like to use the analogy that stress accumulates like dust settling on a glass table. You don't notice it until it is thick and you have to do something about it!

The Causes of Stress

Are you dealing with stress overload in your life? Have you lost the ability to relax and enjoy the moment? Maybe you overreact at the slightest disturbance, or are completely distracted and distant from everything going on around you. Your stress hormones are probably elevated, and the world "out there" seems like a threat to your well-being. When you're stressed, you may be constantly on the defensive against perceived or expected attacks, slowly becoming a victim who's merely reacting to life.

As the pressure mounts, you stop experiencing each day or moment anew. Eventually, you may sense a subtle dissatisfaction or depression, not knowing how it happened or why you feel that way. You might repeat behaviors toward yourself or the world that are not nourishing, making the same choices and responding the same way in relationships. Chronic, unaddressed stress affects your physical, emotional, and mental health; but because its accumulation is so subtle, you may not notice its effects for years.

I can speak from my own experience on this subject. Thanks to having a difficult childhood, by the time I was in my 20s, I was suffering from severe stress and didn't even know it. As a freshman in college (yes, I did eventually go), I first saw the Holmes and Rahe stress scale (a list of stressful life events that contribute to illness) pinned to the wall in my biology professor's office. After I read each item on the chart and tallied up my score, I was surprised to find that I was considered really stressed out.

The funny thing was I didn't *feel* stressed, even though by then my body was showing all the signs. By the time I was an adolescent, I was grinding my teeth and clamping my jaw so tightly in my sleep that I'd cracked several of my molars. I had free-floating anxiety, cried a lot, and had low self-esteem. I skipped school and got in trouble. But that was my "norm," so I didn't see anything unusual about it. I truly didn't notice the effects of stress in my life until they began to dissipate due to my meditation practice. It was as if someone gradually shut off a very loud noise that had been blaring for many years, and the silence and peace became nearly palpable.

○ ○

As it did for me, stress begins early in life for many of us and just keeps on coming. Sometimes the stress is emotional, while other times it's physical; some is mental, and some is caused by your surroundings. Children experience stress when overstimulated by a loud or disruptive environment, such as constantly fighting parents or living with an addict or alcoholic. Stress can come from being bullied or abused and feeling unsafe, or feeling like you don't fit in. It can come from too much pressure to perform a certain way. It can come from being overscheduled and not having enough free time. The same goes for adults, too.

Problems at work cause more health complaints than any other life stressor—more than even financial or family problems. Many Americans view their job as the number one stressor in their lives. According to the American Institute of Stress, over a million workers are absent daily due to stress.

While not everyone will have the same causes of stress, one important element contributes to feeling stressed: the sensation that you have little or no control over things in your life, such as when you have too much to do and not enough time to do it, or too many bills and not enough money. Stress builds up when you want to change another person's behaviors or circumstance; it can come from wanting your children or parents to act in certain ways that they will not, for instance, or from being in a relationship with someone who has self-destructive behaviors and refuses to change. It can come from losing a loved one, having to take on a caregiver's role, or having your relationships suddenly change.

Stress can also come from having expectations or wanting things to go your way. Do you crave a more harmonious relationship with someone, yet all you do is argue? Do you desire a pain-free body, but struggle with pain? Do you want a peaceful world, but keep hearing about war and violence? Human beings are habituated to instant gratification, and stress can be caused by not getting what you want at the speed at which you want it.

War, too, is a major cause of stress, whether it's actual combat, constant fighting in a relationship, or your own mind's struggle with the way things are. Much tension can be caused by uncertainty, too, not knowing with what will happen next. You may think stress has to be accompanied by a thought like, *Gosh, my kids are driving me crazy,* or *I am so late for my appointment,* but in fact, it often accumulates undetected.

You can't always pinpoint the exact causes of stress, and it isn't always accompanied by a conscious feeling of being stressed. Stress can accumulate in your body due to not eating nourishing foods, not digesting food properly, not getting enough sleep, and too much or too little physical activity. It can build up when you are not living in tune with natural daily rhythms, or not outside in nature often enough. It can be caused by living in a polluted environment with excess sound, light, mold, pesticides, chemicals, and bacteria. It can even be caused by hearing bad news or seeing disturbing images in the media. Stress also accumulates when you don't receive the right kind or amount of attention, and when you hang on to toxic relationships.

Stress can be caused by putting off feeling your emotions, vowing to handle them when you "get more time." But as you learned in Week One, it's crucial to feel what you feel as it arises—whether it is pleasant or unpleasant—and to pause for those important moments: to be grateful for life's abundance, to grieve a loss, or even to notice how your body handles difficult moments of pain.

It is important to know that, detected or not, the effects of stress impact each one of us physically, mentally, and emotionally. I learned all about stress when I joined the Army. After I got into some trouble and dropped out of high school, my father insisted I sign up for the military. I complied, thinking it might be fun to become a spy (I always loved solving mysteries!), but because I'd had some minor scrapes with the law, I couldn't get the security clearance I needed. Instead, I was given the opportunity to join the medical corps and train as a specialist in combat stress control for soldiers.

Stress, I found out, actually enhances a soldier's performance in combat—as long as it's controlled. I read about it in a training manual: "Stressors are a fact of combat, and soldiers must face them. It is *controlled* combat stress (when properly focused by training, unit cohesion, and leadership) that gives soldiers the necessary alertness, strength, and endurance to accomplish their mission. *Controlled combat stress* can call forth stress reactions of loyalty, selflessness, and heroism."

I was trained to treat soldiers suffering from the effects of uncontrolled or extreme combat stress. Many suffered from post-traumatic stress disorder (PTSD) caused by situations such as unexpected attacks, witnessing the deaths of friends, being held captive, or feeling guilty after injuring or killing another. My job was to monitor the physical and psychological signs of their stress and to help them adapt so they could return to active duty as soon as possible. (Yet some soldiers *couldn't* go back because of untreatable mental or physical ailments.) It's ironic how thoroughly I'd been taught to identify and deal with all kinds of stress—I could see it everywhere except for in myself!

It's good to remember that you don't have to be a soldier to become highly stressed or suffer from PTSD. And you don't have to wait for a severe wake-up call to do something about your stress.

The Effects of Stress

Stress is sometimes called "the silent killer," because the damage it does isn't always immediately visible and continues to build up over time when left unchecked. As a culture, we have learned to live with its chronic symptoms, even viewing them as commonplace. And though we're getting used to dealing with them, they need to be taken seriously. Excess stress does not always show up in obvious forms, however. Many stresses begin to affect us physically or emotionally in subtle ways.

The list of potential physical complaints from those with stress is long, but here are a few signs: trembling, headaches, jaw clenching, dizziness, ringing in the ears, cold or sweaty hands or feet, frequent infections, rashes, poor digestion and elimination, difficulty breathing, palpitations, and insomnia. You might have nervous habits such as fidgeting, foot tapping, and rapid or mumbled speech. You might experience an increased number of minor accidents, reduced work efficiency, or frequent use of over-the-counter drugs.

Emotional responses include anxiety, fear, panic attacks, depression, anger, aggression, hypervigilance, crying spells, suicidal thoughts, wild mood swings, difficulty concentrating, racing thoughts, memory loss, guilt, and a sense of being overloaded or overwhelmed. You might become overly defensive or suspicious and more judgmental of others, or have difficulty with self-expression and communication. Sometimes stress is expressed in behaviors such as impulse buying, excessive gambling, social withdrawal and isolation, little interest in self-care, obsessive or compulsive behaviors, and other erratic actions. By becoming aware of these signs, you can make changes in your life before the stress turns into something even more difficult to deal with, or causes permanent damage.

The kind of damage that stress does to your body depends on your body's particular weakness—what I call your "strong spot." It's the part of you that can handle the extra load. For instance, stress can cause excessive tissue breakdown, and if your spot is in your joints, this can lead to joint pain or arthritis. If your heart is the spot, it can cause tissue breakdown in the heart and loss of heart muscle. Chronic stress can also cause or exacerbate conditions such as high blood pressure, digestive disorders, diabetes, cancer, infertility, chronic fatigue, fibromyalgia, memory loss, unstable moods, allergies, and suppression of the immune system.

Over my many years of teaching meditation, I have seen the myriad effects of stress in my students. Some arrive with various stress-related complaints, such as insomnia, depression, anxiety, or frustration with their work or personal lives. Others seem to live from crisis to crisis and are taking lots of medication to handle the nagging effects of stress. And some people I see hadn't even known they'd been living with stress until they got a serious wake-up call in the form of an injury, illness, or a loved one leaving.

Fortunately, stress-related conditions often become people's motivation to change their life for the better. When their life is turned upside down, they take a step back and examine who they really are, how they really feel, what's really important to them, and what they really want. That's when they turn to meditation—often viewed as the perfect antidote to stress—and learn to create a restful state of awareness and discover that elusive inner peace. Like my students, you too can wake up and learn to meditate before more stress gets the better of you.

The Physiology of Stress

A couple came to my meditation class and was introduced to the concept of present-moment awareness. When I asked them why they thought being present to the moment was important, the husband replied, "Because that's where the action is!"

This man was a police officer, and when he was called into duty, he relied on his instincts and intuition; his senses and focus sharpened, and he took action. As he described it, "It's like everything gets crystal clear, and I just know what to do without even thinking." A physical and mental state such as this is due to an activation of the nervous system's stress response—the "fight-or-flight" response. Unfortunately, his body's repeated activation of this response had gotten him stuck in a state of chronic stress, unable to relax even after all the action was long over.

The fight-or-flight response was identified in the early 20th century by Harvard physiologist Walter Cannon, and the term is now used to describe the cascade of reactions that ensue anytime we experience a threat, whether from internal worry or external circumstances. Today, we know more about the chemical and hormonal dynamics in the brain and body. The nervous system is made up of two different kinds of response pathways, the *sympathetic* and the *parasympathetic*. The sympathetic pathway, often referred to as the "accelerator," is activated when quick responses are needed, as in fighting or fleeing. The parasympathetic pathway is the "decelerator," and works for situations that don't require an immediate reaction, as in resting and digesting.

When a threat occurs, your accelerator pathway activates to protect you. Sequences of nerve cell firings release an ocean of stress hormones to flood the body. A surge of adrenaline, noradrenaline, cortisol, and other hormones enable you to move and think faster, hit harder, see better, hear more acutely, and jump higher than you could only seconds earlier. Your impulses quicken and all your senses sharpen; even your pupils dilate to sharpen your eyesight so you can scan your environment for threats. Your perception of pain diminishes. Your immune system shifts its focus from addressing and preventing chronic issues to warding off immediate and local antigens.

Whenever your physical survival is actually threatened, this complex response works wonders. It's the same force responsible for mothers lifting cars off their trapped children, soldiers entering combat, and firefighters running into blazing houses to save those trapped inside. But modern-day threats don't often have much to do with actual physical survival. More likely the threats are mundane problems like getting stuck in rush-hour traffic, missing a deadline, bouncing a check, receiving too many e-mails, or having an argument with your boss or spouse. The human nervous system can't distinguish between these threats, so all trigger the fight-or-flight response—a response not particularly helpful in emotionally or mentally stressful situations.

The natural way to discharge the tide of stress hormones and allow the body to return to restful balance is to get physical: fighting or fleeing. But you don't often get the chance to get physical when the response is emotionally or mentally triggered. Instead of slamming the door (the fight response) or walking away (the flight response), you sit with your hands folded in your lap as your boss yells at you, careful to "never let 'em see you sweat." You say "Yes, dear," when your partner is being unreasonable, you deal with your overload of e-mails, you work all night to make a deadline, or you control your frustration while you sit in traffic late for an appointment.

Emotional and mental triggers set off the flood of stress hormones every day; this can have a detrimental effect on your health and well-being and lead to chronic ailments. When the flight-or-fight response has kicked in and you get stressed, you might hold your breath and raise your shoulders up around your ears. Perhaps your stomach ties in knots, and you sweat. Maybe you feel a bit ungrounded, a little explosive, or depressed. When you're not relaxed, it's difficult to maintain awareness of your peaceful center.

It's essential for your mind, body, *and* soul to get your nervous system back on track. One way to discharge the stress and normalize your nervous system is to do a few minutes of aerobic exercise. You can do some jumping jacks, go for a brisk walk, dance to your favorite song, or do a few push-ups (as I would do in the Army when my drill sergeant shouted, "Drop and give me 20, McLean!"). I know, push-ups and jumping jacks may be difficult to do at the office, at school, or in a social situation. And it's not always appropriate to light candles and take a warm bath, or pop open a cold one and put your feet up to relax. I don't suggest you use a meditation practice in the middle of a stressful moment to get your act together or as a Band-Aid for stress either. Instead, to gain relief, you can use the *Peacefinder Exercises* and the *Long, Slow, Deep Breathing* practice you'll find at the end of this week's lesson.

How We Deal with Stress

Sometimes it's easier to ignore the physical or mental signs of stress by telling ourselves "It's all good," then eating, drinking, or shopping our stress away. Perhaps we watch TV to forget about our work or personal demands rather than handle them. And some of us deal with our stress with alcohol, caffeine, sugar, or drugs (whether recreational, over-the-counter, or prescription), rather than making lifestyle changes to alleviate its source.

You may have been convinced by advertisements that it is normal to take a pill or other aid for even the simplest bodily functions—going to the bathroom, sleeping, waking up, having sex, or digesting food. Other popular prescriptions include pills for controlling anxiety, blood pressure, cholesterol, diabetes, indigestion, allergies, and general aches and pain. Mood elevators and antidepressants are prescribed even more often. Prescriptions written for antidepressants jumped from 13 million in 1996 to 164 million in 2008.

These conditions deemed "chronic" that are so often treated with pharmaceuticals are the exact indicators that the mind and body are out of balance, likely due to or exacerbated by stress. At first it may seem easier to reach for an aspirin to get rid of a headache, take Zoloft to alleviate your bad mood, and pop an Ambien for a good night's sleep. But is it really? These medications' side effects can affect the subtle balance in the body and cause even more stress.

Instead, there are many healthy ways to handle stress. You might turn to creative outlets, spend more time with your family, get massages, go for walks, or commit to exercising more and eating better. Keep in mind that the most effective, natural way for the body to get back to balance is by getting a good night's sleep. I suggest you aim for that, though it can be difficult to attain for those who are too stressed-out. Luckily, meditation has not only been proven to alleviate the stress that causes sleep interruptions, it also serves to give the body some deep rest. (You'll learn more about the importance of good sleep in Week Eight.)

A Meditator's Story: A New Lease on Life

Ken was a software programmer for one of the top 50 companies in the U.S. He felt lucky to be able to work from home, and he enjoyed his job. It was, however, seasonally stressful. He thought nothing of it until he was diagnosed with an irregular heartbeat, a condition called atrial fibrillation, or "A-fib." Although A-fib isn't life threatening on its own, it can lead to complications such as stroke, blood clots, and heart failure.

At the time Ken started meditating with me, he was taking four prescription medications for his condition. He told me, "One of the suggestions my doctor made was to reduce my stress. I didn't want to give up my 14-year job as a programmer, so I started researching my options. At first, I bought a heavy boxing bag with the idea that punching something could help relieve stress. Then my wife suggested that I learn meditation."

Ken attended my weekend meditation class and began practicing silent meditation every day. He quickly found that his stress levels were reduced and his mood brightened. He was even able to stop episodes of his heart irregularity by meditating when the symptoms came on. He said that after one such episode, "I tested my pulse and it was normal—no A-fib, no arrhythmia, just a normal strong pulse." But in spite of his altered mood and decreased A-fib events, his blood pressure skyrocketed over the next year. "When it hit 170/100, I decided to give up the job. Even though the company had great benefits, I didn't want to leave a widow to collect death benefits."

Ken kept up with his meditation practice, which continued to improve his well-being by reducing stress. He found his creativity, too, and engaged in creative-writing practices. He sought out other natural approaches, receiving acupuncture treatments and adopting dietary changes based on traditional Chinese medicine. He eventually lost more than 50 pounds and now takes only one prescription medication. He's had one A-fib episode in almost two years. He credits meditation with opening the doors to his healthier, more fulfilling life.

Meditation and the Restful Awareness Response

An ounce of prevention is worth a pound of cure—so don't wait for the stress to build and become the disease, the divorce, or the diagnosis. Meditation is a great preventive tool as well as one of the best ways to reduce stress and give your mind and body the attention it needs. Meditation provides a period of restfulness often comparable to what you get in deep sleep. It also shifts your mind and body into what is called the "restful awareness response"—basically, the opposite of the fight-or-flight response.

When you meditate, your parasympathetic nervous system is activated. Your brain waves settle into a more relaxed, aware, and coherent state. Your body returns to a smoother-running, restful response; and your oxygen consumption, heart rate, and blood pressure all decrease. Meditation is the only activity known to reduce blood lactate, a marker of stress and anxiety. It also increases levels of melatonin (a hormone that supports the immune system and regulates sleep cycles) and "feel-good hormones" like endorphins and serotonin.

Although you will usually start your meditation practice by paying attention to your body and your breath, your awareness of those things will quickly decrease. Soon, your awareness transcends your mind's activity—with all of its fears, anxieties, and strategies—and loses track of how your body is responding, as you dive into the silence that underlies all activity.

Like in sleep, you gain deep rest in meditation. Your body and mind take advantage of the opportunity to purify and get rid of built-up toxicity, including undigested matter, emotions, experiences, and stress. Wholeness and balance are restored and the interconnection between the body, mind, and soul is optimized.

Some say when you meditate, you directly experience your soul, the aspect of you that is naturally stress-free and peaceful. When you come out of meditation, you bring some of that awareness with you. With regular meditation and reduced stress, your perception of the world begins to alter and before you know it, the world becomes a friendlier place to live. You feel calm, vital, and balanced; eventually, you find yourself living a peaceful, soul-centered life.

Meditation: It's Not What You Think

Even though I say it's okay to have thoughts in meditation, some people think they're meditating incorrectly when they have them. This is not true. Spontaneous thoughts are a natural part of meditation. You can't stop thoughts by resisting them or by thinking about stopping them. It's the nature of the mind to think. Your job in meditation is to notice when you get distracted by mental activity; then, without judgment, simply move your attention back to the focus of your practice. It's perfectly normal to get caught up in stories or have thoughts about what you're doing, such as *This feels good* or *Isn't it time to stop meditating yet?* When you become aware of your internal dialogue, remember to simply, kindly, return your attention and awareness to your breath or whatever your focus is in your meditation.

Some type A personalities like to meditate with a notebook by their side, so if and when inspiration strikes, they can stop meditating and write down their insights. I do not suggest doing this. If I have a thought in meditation that I feel is important, it's usually there when I come out of meditation.

There are thoughts that may compel you to take action, such as *I should really return that call* or *Did I leave the water on?* They are to be met the same way as any other thoughts: with a kind, gentle refocusing. You are changing your relationship to your mental activity, cultivating responsiveness rather than reactivity to your mind. This is helpful in meditation *and* in life.

You might also have the thought to stop meditating. Maybe it doesn't feel like it's working, or you think you have too much mental activity (often called the "monkey mind"). But don't stop. Dealing with the mind is something that athletes have to learn to deal with, too. Long-distance bicyclists and runners know that the first obstacle to their training is their mind's obstinate narrative saying things like *It's not the best time to be doing this, Maybe I should do it tomorrow instead,* or *There's no point—I'm not seeing any progress anyway.* Athletes learn to keep going, even when the mind protests.

Athletes also find that keeping their attention in the present moment is essential. When athletes focus on the future, like thinking about miles ahead when they're only on the first, they often find it makes their training and practice much more draining and stressful. Bringing their focus back to the present moment—on their movement, breath, and rhythm—helps them access the vitality they need and continue more easily.

The lessons of these athletes' experiences—staying with the training while keeping their attention in the present moment—are easily translatable to meditation. When athletes keep going beyond the protests of their mind, for instance, they eventually experience more ease and even a peak moment like a "runner's high." This blissful state is the result of the release of endorphins and other brain chemicals. You can feel a similar "meditator's high" by staying committed to your practice, even when your mind tells you it's time to stop. Don't actively seek this experience in meditation; it is a natural state that you reach only when you practice without effort and stick with it.

○ ○

Thoughts in meditation occur because it's the nature of the mind to think, but it's also one of three ways that the body uses to release stress. (The other two ways are through emotions and physical sensations, which we will discuss shortly.) It's important to know that while thoughts are often an indication that stress is being released, the actual content of the thoughts doesn't have anything to do with the type of stress being released. For instance, let's say that while you're meditating, you begin to think about how to solve an issue at work. This activity of the mind—thinking about work—indicates that you're releasing stress. However, the content of the thought—work—doesn't usually correlate with the source of the stress being released. You could be releasing stress totally unrelated to work, maybe something that's deep in your nervous system.

The deep rest your mind and body attains in meditation can lead to an unraveling of undigested emotions, too. When your mind settles down, your body follows, and stored emotions are released. You might find that you get tearful, experience bliss, or feel fearful or anxious, all for no apparent reason. These emotional releases indicate that you're purifying suppressed, unexpressed, or repressed emotions that have left residue in your body. When an emotion arises, don't interpret it; resist the urge to dramatize it or tell yourself a story about why you have it. Instead, simply feel the emotion as energy moving through your body.

Emotions coming up in meditation indicate that you are releasing something that you didn't fully experience at the time it happened. Unlike with thoughts, in the case of emotions, there is a correlation between past emotions and the one that is being released in meditation. You've probably heard the phrase, *Issues in your tissues*. Well, meditation is a great way to let go of those issues easily.

The tendency is to ask yourself, *What happened that made me feel this way?* You might try to link it to something that happened either in the past or that is happening around you as you meditate—perhaps you blame your irritation on your neighbors being too noisy, or think you feel anxiety because you forgot to send an e-mail. Instead of assigning a reason for the emotion, simply feel the sensations in your body. Let the emotion move through you, and bear witness to it. Emotions are energy in motion—they should quickly pass. Allow the sensation to dissipate without judgment, then gently return to the focus of your meditation.

The third way that the body releases stress is in the form of a physical sensation. You can feel restless, twitchy, tingly, hot, cool, or numb. You can feel very big or very small, very heavy or light enough to float. Some people feel movement, while others feel perfectly still. Where and what you experience physically, unlike with thoughts, *does* relate to that particular physical area. Your body may be trying to regain its balance, for instance. If you have some tingling, it could be you've just released some long-held stress in that area of your body, or your circulation has normalized. General twitching is often a general release of your entire nervous system. However, if you feel pain during meditation, pay attention to it rather than ignoring it. Feel it with a nonjudgmental attitude. Don't go telling yourself a story about the pain; simply feel it . . . explore the sensations . . . bear witness to it. It should subside with your awareness. When the meditation is over, you will often find the pain is gone.

Stress release in meditation is a gentle process; you don't have to relive any mental, physical, or emotional trauma in order for it to be released. I like to say that most sensations in meditation correlate with stress moving out or some sort of purification. Thoughts, physical sensations, and emotions will always be a part of your practice, so it is important to learn to "be with" them as they arise. As you continue your practice, you will become more and more familiar with the natural silence of your mind that also accompanies them. By meditating regularly, the inward focus and ability to stay with the practice no matter what arises will become easier and more comfortable.

Practices and Exercises to Cultivate Peace

Peacefinder Exercises

When you feel trapped in a situation and are under stress, there are a few quick exercises you can do to find some peace. No one even has to know. Practice the exercises below as you read them; each one takes less than a minute. They're great to have on hand when you need to refresh your attitude or shift your body's response.

— *Close your eyes:* You can usually close your eyes without being noticed, even if just for half a minute. Try it now. The outside world takes a backseat while you go within. You almost instantly regain a sense of balance and relaxation.

— *Feel your breath:* You can find inner peace with your eyes open, too. Focus your attention on your breath as you did last week. Slowly take in a deep breath through your nose, and let it out slowly through your nose. Pause for two seconds, then repeat. Holding the breath after you exhale helps counteract stress patterns of shallow breathing or holding the breath in. In, out, hold, repeat.

— *Count your breaths*: Eyes open or closed, it might help to silently count your breaths. In, count one; out, count two. Count your breaths all the way to ten. The mind might wander, but simply keep bringing your focus back to your breath and counting. This helps calm your nervous system.

— *30-second body scan:* Bring your attention to how your body feels, sitting or standing, right where you are at this moment. With your eyes open or closed, scan your body from the top down, front and back, relaxing as you go. Relax your forehead, your eyes, your mouth, your tongue, your jaw. Lower your shoulders and relax your belly. Bring your attention to your hands, then your feet. In less than a minute, you can feel better from the inside out.

— *Say a prayer or affirmation:* Silently repeating a prayer or an affirmation can immediately shift your focus from a stressful situation to peace. *All is well, I'm doing the best I can,* and *This too shall pass* are good examples. You can also choose a single word, like *Peace, Trust,* or *Calm.* Silently, slowly repeat the chosen word, phrase, or prayer seven times.

— *Slow down:* Do one thing at a time, just a little slower than usual. Get up from your chair more deliberately or walk a bit more slowly—you'll find that this helps ease the tension, brings you back to the present moment, and relaxes your mind and body.

— *Pay attention to each one of your senses*: What are you hearing in this moment? What are you feeling? What are you seeing? What do you taste? What do you smell? By paying attention to your senses, your focus can shift back to the present moment just enough to relieve stress.

— *Smile:* Give yourself a smile. Smiling releases endorphins that reduce stress and help you feel better. Studies have shown that even faking a smile can lead to feeling happier. Even if it feels strange at first, make it a point to smile more often.

— *Excuse yourself:* If you're unhappy in the moment, or if you're around people who are unhappy, the discomfort can be contagious. Whenever you notice signals of stress in your body, simply excuse yourself with something like, "I've got to get back to a project," and walk away. That project is your inner peace. Go outside, back to your desk, or head to the bathroom. Once there, use one of the above techniques.

Long, Slow, Deep Breathing

Long, Slow, Deep Breathing is a perfect complement to the *Sitting Meditation* you'll learn this week. This simple, natural exercise relaxes you and slows you down, yet also energizes you. When stressed, your breath becomes rapid and shallow, and sometimes you forget to breathe at all. When you take long, slow, deep breaths through your nose, it sends a signal to your mind and body to shift into the parasympathetic response. Some studies suggest that slow, deep breathing is as effective in reducing anxiety as antidepressants are.

Long, Slow, Deep Breathing enhances your self-awareness, helps you regain peace when stressed, and is a great way to get a natural lift. Blood circulation in the diaphragm stimulates and enlivens the entire body—which is why it's best not to do this practice too close to bedtime. You can do this exercise for up to ten minutes at a time.

This week, you'll do this exercise for three minutes before the *Sitting Meditation*. Here's how:

— Find a way to time yourself (but don't use an alarm that you will need to get up to turn off).

— Sit in a comfortable position, resting your hands in your lap.

— You can keep your eyes open, but you might want to close them. You can also keep them slightly opened, or "capped." (Capping is a practice of maintaining a soft, unfocused, downward gaze directed two to three feet in front of you. It helps integrate silence into activity.)

— Give yourself a few moments to relax your body from head to toe. Soften your belly.

— Inhale slowly through the nostrils, filling your abdominal area first, then the chest cavity, then the clavicle area. Visualize expanding your body in 360 degrees as you inhale.

— Once your lungs are completely filled, hold your breath only for a few seconds while pressing your shoulders back and expanding your chest, so the pressure of your breath on your diaphragm can be felt.

— Exhale slowly through the nostrils, beginning with the clavicle area, then the chest cavity, and then the abdominal area, contracting your navel toward your spine to clear your lungs completely. Hold the breath out for a few seconds.

— As you continue to use your muscles in your belly, chest, and shoulders, you'll begin to feel the sensation of a natural bellows-like motion in the diaphragm. Never force an exhale or inhale.

— Continue with your long, slow, deep breaths; keeping the length of the inhales and exhales equal; and pausing for a count or two in between breaths. You may average five to nine full breaths per minute.

Before You Begin the Sitting Meditation Practice

Week One's exercises prepared you for this week's *Sitting Meditation*, one of the oldest, most time-honored meditation practices around. My first introduction to this form of meditation was shortly after I graduated from college. My friends and I visited a Zen Center near Boston, Massachusetts, and we were taught *zazen*, a Japanese word that means sitting meditation. A teacher in a black robe took us aside and gave us some brief instruction in the walking meditation, two ways to sit on the *zafu* (a round meditation cushion), and the position in which to hold our hands during meditation. We learned some ceremonial bows, too. We were given the instruction to pay attention to our breath but nothing more about what to think or feel, or what to expect, only to sit still and straight and not to move until we heard the bell.

The sitting meditation that follows, however, is a bit different. You can move if you want to, and it is accoutrement-free—there are no special chairs, cushions, chimes, or outfits required. All you need is your willingness to do it and a way to time yourself.

○ ○

There are a few things that I'd like you to keep in mind. I covered some of this in the Introduction, but want to remind you of them here.

First, although you might have ideas of what meditation should be like, leave them all behind. Expectations only make it more difficult to meditate. People like to be doing something in order to feel like they're getting somewhere, but the opposite is true in meditation. There is no *doing*. It's a practice of being still in order to make progress.

Remember that you don't have to quiet your mind completely to successfully meditate. Just get comfortable with the fact that you will have thoughts, and that doesn't mean you're doing it wrong. It is also normal to feel restless, bored, emotional, or sleepy. And though you can't *do* anything to quiet your mind, your mind will eventually settle down. You can't go wrong unless you give up or try too hard.

Traditionally, the first meditation of the day is in the early morning. Sit in meditation before the day gets going, so you'll be sure to get it in before you get distracted. (At The Chopra Center, they say "R.P.M.," short for "rise, pee, meditate." Easy to remember.) Ideally, the second meditation is in the evening between work and dinner, what I call the Happy Hour meditation. Don't meditate on a full stomach, as digestion seems to activate the body and the mind. If you do need to eat, try to wait at least an hour to meditate. Another good time is before lunch. Your body likes rhythm, so develop a meditation schedule and stick with it.

Although meditation may relax you and is proven to improve sleeping habits, you shouldn't do it too close to bedtime. Some practices are okay to do before bed, but the *Sitting Meditation* and the *Long, Slow Deep Breathing* could give you energy and keep you up longer than you like. Try to start meditation at least three hours before bedtime.

It's important to keep track of the time while meditating. You can use the vibrate mode of your cell phone's alarm or download a meditation app for your smart phone or computer. You can also peek at your watch or a clock from time to time. Do not use an alarm that you will have to jump up to turn off. Predetermine the amount of time you will practice and stick with it, no matter what your mind says (unless there's an emergency, and checking your e-mail is *not* an emergency).

You might want to get up in the middle of your meditation because you feel restless and bored or think, *This isn't working,* or *I have a great idea!* But if you sit through these impulses, you'll release a great amount of stress and will feel really refreshed after.

Although it may be a romantic notion to sit outside on a mountaintop and meditate, it isn't always practical. The ideal can be any quiet place indoors. Designate an area where you'll be able to meditate regularly, such as a comfortable chair in your bedroom or on your favorite cushion on the floor. If you can't seem to find the perfect spot, don't let that stop you from meditating. One of my favorite places to practice is my car, because I can always find some alone time there (obviously not when I'm driving!). You'll often find me in a parking lot, eyes closed, meditating between appointments. I meditate on planes, in libraries, and in churches. You too can meditate anywhere you feel safe and will be undisturbed.

Wherever you decide to meditate, turn off all electronics and other sources of noise when possible. Put your phone's ringer on silent, and turn off your TV, iPod, and other devices. Meditation is a practice of turning your attention inward, and music can charm your awareness outward, so don't listen to anything while meditating, even if it's called "meditation music." White noise is okay. Put a "do not disturb" sign on your door and ask those around not to bother you during this time. Leave your animals outside or in another room. Do whatever you can to limit distractions. If you are interrupted in the middle of your practice, go back and finish up whatever time remains.

Many people want to know if they have to sit cross-legged on the floor. The answer is no; although there are traditional meditation postures, they are not necessary to use. Sit however you like, just be sure you're comfortable while sitting with your spine relatively straight. If you decide to sit on the floor, you can lift your rear off the ground a little by sitting on a cushion or a pillow folded in half; this makes it easier on your back. You might sit "Indian style" or with one leg folded in front of the other on the floor. Don't try a complicated position unless you are really comfortable.

You can lie down before or after, but do not lie down while you meditate. Many people want to, but I suggest that you don't. You've trained yourself to fall asleep in this position for years. Lying down makes the whole process one of a sleeping meditation or napping, which is a different thing altogether. The only exception to this rule is if you have to lie down due to a medical condition.

Rest your hands on your lap, on your knees, or on the arms of the chair. Palms up, palms down, folded, however you like; find what feels comfortable for you. Your head can tilt down very slightly, chin in. Sit still with your eyes closed or capped. If you feel the need to open your eyes during meditation, do so, then close them again right away.

Read through the *Sitting Meditation* instructions a few times. Keep in mind that it's a practice. Let go of expectations, be kind to yourself, and stay committed to the program.

Sitting Meditation

You can do the *Sitting Meditation* successfully the very first time. The measure of success is to simply do it, letting what happens, happen. Don't try to have a certain experience; instead, approach this practice with a beginner's mind, a mind that is free of preconceptions, expectations, judgments, and prejudices (you'll learn more about this next week).

The difference between this week's *Sitting Meditation* practice and last week's *Breath Awareness* is that this week's meditation is done in a comfortable seated position. It's an essential part of the 8-week program. Many of my students say that this meditation is their primary daily meditation practice.

This week, practice this meditation for 10 to 15 minutes, twice a day, for a total of 30 minutes a day. Follow the instructions below with an innocent, open attitude and a relaxed body. Here's how:

— Sit comfortably with your spine upright but not rigid. Close or cap your eyelids.

— Sit still, but if you feel uncomfortable, feel free to move a little. Yes, you can scratch an itch, but don't distract yourself by trying to repeatedly find the "perfect" position.

— Tuck your chin in slightly and lengthen the back of your neck. Do not strain in any way.

— Scan your body with your awareness from head to toe to be sure it's relaxed, as you did last week.

— Give yourself five slow, deep breaths through the nose. Then let your breath return to its natural rhythm.

— Take a moment to notice the various sounds in your environment. Welcome them, and do not resist them. Nothing is a distraction in this meditation.

— Bring your attention again to your breath as you breathe through your nose. Observe your breath's natural movement and flow, without controlling or manipulating it in any way. It may get deeper or shallower, slow down, speed up, or pause for a moment. Simply feel its sensations.

— Thoughts, feelings, judgments, or impressions from the outside world may arise as you sit. Notice them, but don't try to stop them; instead, simply refocus on your breath. Remember to be kind to yourself. Don't try too hard.

— You may realize that you've been daydreaming or planning for a while, too. This is normal. Don't worry or stress; instead, simply refocus on your breath.

— Some thoughts seem fascinating, but no matter how charming those thoughts might be, don't indulge them. You can think about them later, outside of meditation.

— You may notice that your attention is on a physical sensation of some kind. Again, simply refocus on your breath.

— Since you are training your awareness to be focused, it doesn't matter how often you lose your focus. Thoughts coming and going have nothing to do with how deep your meditation is. You're doing it right even if you find you have to refocus over and over again. Stay with it.

— Keep a relaxed attitude. There's no need to force your attention, as you would in concentration. Simply welcome whatever experience comes. There's nothing to figure out, no need to try hard, and nothing to control.

— Continue for 15 minutes (or whatever length of time you have predetermined).

— When your time is up, keep your eyes closed, take your attention off your breath, and sit in the silence for at least a few minutes. You can lie down or gently stretch your body. Do not jump up. Instead, take your time coming out of your meditation.

— After at least two minutes, give yourself a smile, and slowly open your eyes.

Schedule of Practices and Exercises

Week Two: Suggested Daily Practices	
AM	Long, Slow, Deep Breathing: 3 Minutes
	Sitting Meditation: 12 Minutes
PM	Body Awareness: 3 Minutes
	Sitting Meditation: 12 Minutes

Additional Awareness Exercises	
Anytime	Peacefinder Exercises
	Body Awareness
	Breath Awareness

Insights for Success

During these exercises and practices, there's no right or wrong way to feel, as every practice period will be different depending on your life circumstances and ever-changing physical and emotional states. This includes how you slept, what you ate, what your personal interactions were that day, and so on. And naturally you'll like some experiences better than others.

You might begin to expect your meditation to go a certain way based on previous ones. Yet it's important to treat each meditation without preconceptions or expectations. Some meditations will surprise you!

Even if you don't feel as if you went very deep in your meditation, your opinion might not matter. When you meditate easily and effortlessly, you naturally reach a deep state of rest. If you were electronically monitored in a lab, you'd see that your body and mind were in a state of deep rest. That's why at the end of the meditation period, it is essential to sit in stillness for at least two minutes with your eyes closed. Even if you get the urge to jump up right away, don't. Give yourself a few minutes to adjust, coming from the deep rest and silence back into your active life.

Don't judge the effectiveness of your meditation by the experiences you have during meditation. Instead, look for the effectiveness in your daily life: less stress, more focus and clarity, more self-awareness, and more confidence. If there is a goal to meditation, in the broadest sense, it is to have a better life—a transformed, soul-centered life.

Enjoy your week!

○ ○ ○

FREEDOM: BEGIN WITH A BEGINNER'S MIND

"Look at everything as though you were seeing it for the first time or last time. Then your time on earth will be filled with glory."

— BETTY SMITH, AUTHOR OF *A TREE GROWS IN BROOKLYN*

In last week's lesson, your focus was on how to find peace or return to peace when you are stressed. This requires being present in the moment and being self-aware, which are qualities you've been cultivating. Some days you may have looked forward to your *Sitting Meditation* and other days it may have been more difficult to practice. I encourage you to keep your commitment. It works even if you don't think it does.

This week's focus is cultivating the *beginner's mind*, a way of perceiving things with an open attitude. We've all been in this mind-set before, when we were experiencing something awesome and inspiring for the first time. Recall one of these events now. Maybe it was something you saw, like the vast Grand Canyon or the glow of Sedona's red rocks. Perhaps it was something you felt, like the soft fur of a puppy or kitten, or something you heard, such as a live orchestral performance. Was it something you tasted, like a perfect chocolate truffle or freshly cut pineapple? Perhaps you smelled wild night jasmine or a fresh ocean breeze. Whatever it was, you met it with your beginner's mind, a state of complete freedom from preconceived ideas. Nothing got in the way of your experience, and it delighted you.

Beginner's mind is a peaceful perspective to have both in meditation and in life, and is an essential ingredient to being soul-centered. As you let go of ideas, judgments, and expectations, the simplest things appear new and exciting—even if you've experienced them many times before. To cultivate the beginner's mind, you'll continue your meditation practice from last week, and add two new exercises: *Delectable Eating* and *Walking Without Labels*.

Empty Your Cup

I first learned about beginner's mind during my training at the Zen Mountain Center, but you don't have to be a Buddhist to have a beginner's mind. Siddhartha Gautama, also known as the Buddha, wasn't a Buddhist either. Brought up Hindu, he renounced his religion and went looking for freedom from ideas and beliefs. He wanted to experience life directly and went on a quest for the beginner's mind.

The following Zen *koan* (wisdom story) illustrates the importance of the beginner's mind:

> A Zen master received a university professor who was visiting the master's monastery to learn about Zen. The master served the professor tea. He poured his visitor's cup full, and then he kept on pouring. The professor watched the overflow until he could no longer restrain himself. "The cup is overfull! No more will go in!"
>
> "Like this cup," the master said, "you are full of your own opinions and expectations. How can I show you Zen unless you first empty your cup?"

Many of us are like the visiting professor, searching for wisdom with a mind already full of expectations and judgments about what is right or wrong, true or untrue. It is overflowing with what we already know. As you practice meditation with a welcoming, nonresistant, innocent attitude, you cultivate a beginner's mind. This perspective is helpful both in and out of meditation; your inner monologue of *I know what that is* or *I know what's supposed to happen next* begins to quiet down.

With a beginner's mind you let go of being an expert and walk through the world with fresh eyes: open, innocent, and with a childlike curiosity. You empty your cup, making room to receive life as it meets your senses. This allows you to approach your life and your experiences without preconceived ideas, concepts, or notions about *any of it*. You experience things as if for the first time, freely, without letting the labels and ideas get in the way of what you experience while you're experiencing it.

Beginner's mind is similar to present-moment awareness from Week One but with an important difference: With present-moment awareness, you address the mind's wanderings into the past and future, bringing the focus back to the present moment. With beginner's mind, you address your mind's tendency to label and already *know* every experience, bringing your focus back to what you're actually experiencing instead of your idea of it.

Ideas vs. Direct Experience

Recently, I was walking in the hills around Phoenix and enjoying the riot of bright orange, yellow, and purple wildflowers covering the hillside. I walked by a bush I wanted to hug, because it was so vibrant in its full bloom. My friend, responding to my excitement, said, "Don't you just love that Mexican bird of paradise?" Down the path, a tiny bird, beautifully speckled, was sitting on a tree branch singing. It took my breath away, but evoked my friend's response, "Oh, look! A cactus wren . . ." Although the names of these things were interesting, the experience of the flowers and the presence of the bird were even more sublime.

Your mind naturally wants to identify and catalog all you experience, which was what my friend was doing. The mind operates by naming, labeling, separating, and often judging everyone and everything you come in contact with. Because you categorize them, you think you know them. This becomes a habitual way of responding to people and the environment—instead of making you more familiar with things, it disconnects you from actually experiencing them.

One summer a few years ago, the peach trees in our backyard were loaded with an abundance of fruit. I *love* fresh peaches. My husband and I were delighted as we harvested them and brought them into the kitchen, spreading them out on the counters. The smell was intoxicating. The colors of the peaches were vibrant shades of reds and yellows, and they were covered with the fuzziest skins. I learned to make peach pie, peach tarts, peach chutneys, and peach smoothies. As I peeled the skins and cut the fruit, some of the pits came out easily while others were stubborn. Each peach I bit into was mouthwatering, juicy, fresh, and satisfying.

You might be thinking that you know all about these peaches I'm describing. Perhaps you can picture them or have tasted some just like mine. But no matter how much detail I give you about these peaches, or how much you think you know them, you can't have the experience of them through words or ideas. The only way to actually know these peaches is to taste them for yourself.

For many of us, the ideas we hold have actually replaced the direct experience of the ingredients of our lives. We've had years of gathering knowledge from school, church, books, TV, movies, magazines, and the Internet. We have preconceived notions from tradition, religion, and culture, prejudices from our personal history and how we were raised. We collect ideas (often they are *ideals,* too) about all sorts of things, such as romance, relaxation, glamour, love, emotions, God, spirituality, wealth, holidays, and even the perfect children. These ideas of our life often overshadow the actual reality. Ideas become the touchstone, a false substitute for the actual experience they represent.

Words are also substitutes for direct experience. You may think you know something because you know the word that represents it. Words can become labels that put distance between you and what they represent, robbing you of a direct connection with whatever it is you're experiencing. This applies to feelings *(happy, sad, mad, glad)* and to things *(table, chair, peach, sky)*. If I say the word *raven* or *buttercup* or *strawberry*, you'd "know" what I was talking about; but if an actual raven, buttercup, or strawberry were to appear in front of your eyes, would you fully experience it? Or would you label it and experience your *idea* of it because you already *know* what you're looking at?

When we refrain from labeling, we give ourselves an opportunity to experience everything as it is. When looking at ourselves, another, a situation, or a thing with a beginner's mind, there is an opportunity to have a clear, direct experience of reality as it is, rather than just a label or an idea of it.

Judgments and Assumptions

Sometimes we label people by what they look like, or by their position or possessions, without getting to know anything more about them. A prejudice, or prejudgment, is an assumption you make about someone or something before having adequate knowledge of them. As you slowly read the following list of labels, be aware of what your mind does: *priest, policeman, Democrat, Republican, tree hugger, terrorist, welfare mother, retiree, schoolteacher, thief, millionaire, farmer, grandmother, rapist, politician, CEO, drug addict, nurse.*

Maybe you have been the one who's been prejudged and know how strange and hurtful that can be—I certainly have. Prejudgment is another form of labeling that keeps someone from seeing who or what is actually in front of them, whether it's a person, a place, a thing, or even a belief system or religion. Assumptions and prejudices can often be subtle or hidden. They may keep us from relating to one another, as illustrated by the following story:

A woman is traveling to work downtown on a train when a man gets on with his three kids. The man takes a seat, but his kids are running wildly, wrestling with each other, knocking into the woman, causing her papers to fly and her coffee to spill. The father seems oblivious, as he stares blankly at the floor.

The woman shoots the man a dirty look and asks accusingly, "What is wrong with you? Can't you control your kids better?" The man looks up and notices what's going on. He tells the woman, "I don't know what to do. The children and I just came from their mother's funeral." Now the woman shrinks in her seat, her assumptions embarrassingly revealed.

You can never know what others have experienced, where they've been, what's going on in their mind, or what they believe in, simply by looking at them. This can cause misunderstandings in relationships and a lack of intimacy. It's best to take an attitude of *I don't know*. You can always ask before you speak, and if you hear yourself saying "I assumed that . . . ," then that's a cue you've stepped away from beginner's mind.

The Know-It-All Mind

The opposite of a beginner's mind is a *know-it-all mind*. This mental habit is developed due to feeling unsafe with uncertainty. It helps people feel secure, even if it is simply by being the keeper of ideas and facts. You can easily spot the know-it-all mind. Have you ever been in a conversation with someone who interrupts you by repeatedly saying, "I know! I know!" when he or she couldn't possibly know what you're talking about? Similarly, this know-it-all mind can be the first obstacle you meet in yourself when you begin your meditation practice. You may think you already *know* what you are supposed to experience, feel, and do.

This reminds me of a truck driver from the East Coast who was referred to me because of the stress and anxiety in his life. He spent most of his day in traffic and had labels for all kinds of customers: the good ones, the bad ones, the shady ones, and so on. In the course of our conversation, he told me that he knew all about meditation, though he hadn't ever experienced it.

As I told him about the effects of stress and how meditation could ease his anxiety, he didn't seem to be listening; perhaps it was because he already "knew." He also "knew" the kind of experience he was "supposed" to be having during meditation, so it was a challenge for him to follow instructions, even just being kind to himself and being without expectations. Finally, I guided him through a breath-counting practice to give his know-it-all mind something to do. When the meditation was over, he was astonished by how quickly he was able to relax and surrender to the process. I believe if he keeps at it, meditation will help him develop a beginner's mind.

○ ○

When you have expectations about how things will turn out in life, those expectations can rob you of a direct experience and limit the possibilities available. The same goes for meditation. When you have ideas of how your meditation experience should go or whether it's "worth it" or "good enough," those thoughts can only get in your way.

Expectations can disappoint us when they're not fulfilled and can certainly frustrate a new meditator. For instance, one woman said to me, "I want to have a meditation session at home on my own, like I did with you in class." She thought she was doing it wrong at home, and she wanted it to be better or different. This expectation kept her attention focused on an idea and trying to have it go a certain way, rather than what she was actually experiencing. It kept her mentally engaged, looking for a certain experience; this kept her mind from settling, so it was a no-win situation.

When you meditate with a beginner's mind and let the experiences come naturally, it can be a blissful experience, beyond your ideas of what can happen. One of my students described it this way: "It was like standing on top of a mountain and seeing the whole world laid out at my feet. I felt I was a part of something much larger than myself, and at the same time knew it was always within me. I can still see the image I had when I opened my eyes and looked out the window after meditating for the first time: swirling pinks and purples, the rocks against that dark and moody sky. It was as if the world had polished itself just for me."

The expectations I had when I first learned to meditate dealt with how I was supposed to act outside of the practice. I thought I was supposed to be cool, calm, and collected, even if I didn't feel that way. I even put a bumper sticker on my car that read, IT'S ALL GOOD. This is an example of what some call a *spiritual bypass,* which means that I pretended to feel something I didn't actually feel—it was only what I thought I *should* feel as someone who meditated. My bumper sticker wasn't true—it wasn't all good. I didn't like certain situations, I still got mad, I still judged people, and that was the way it was. But I had the idea that people who meditate should be peaceful, and this idea kept me from being honest and true to myself. The know-it-all mind leaves little room for what is really happening, and this can cause a lot of stress.

Labeling Your Emotions

We not only label people, places, and things, we also label our inner experiences—specifically our emotions. Initially, this labeling can help some people identify and sort out their emotions as they arise, especially if they've become detached from how they feel. Ultimately, however, labeling gets in the way of actually experiencing emotions.

When we were children, we were often told not to feel something: *Don't be afraid. Honey, stop crying. Let's not get angry now.* Since we wanted to please those around us, we figured out which emotions to feel and which not to feel. Our reference point shifted from our own integrity—how we actually felt inside—to an external idea of how we "should" feel. This could get confusing: we might have known the label of what we were supposed to feel in a certain situation, yet we didn't actually feel it. Then, as we matured, rather than actually feeling our emotions, we imposed on ourselves the ideas we learned early on of how we should feel and how that feeling should be expressed, repressing the feelings that actually arose.

Have you ever heard someone say "I don't know how to feel about this" or "I don't know what I'm feeling"? It's not necessary to know how you feel; it's only necessary to feel how you feel. Feelings are for *feeling*, not for *knowing*. With beginner's mind, you feel your emotions.

In relationships, this dynamic of knowing rather than feeling can be a problem. Not long ago, for instance, a woman came to me in the hopes that meditation would improve her marriage of ten years. She told me that she knew what it meant to be romantic and affectionate, and her husband was neither. She said he was doing his best to please her by often holding her hand or putting his arm around her, and they had a decent sex life. She also said they spent a lot of time together, eating breakfast every morning and playing Scrabble most evenings when he got home from work. But in spite of this, she didn't think that his actions were romantic or affectionate, so she wasn't fulfilled by the relationship.

While he was holding her hand, she wanted him to tell her she looked beautiful. While he was playing Scrabble with her, she wanted him to plan their next vacation. When he took her out to dinner, she wanted him to buy her jewelry. She missed enjoying the experience of him being sweetly present with her, because she had an idea that romance and love looked another way. She missed the richness of his actions and was unable to respond emotionally to him. After she learned to meditate, however, she was able to establish a beginner's mind when it came to feeling her feelings and experiencing the attention her husband actually gave her.

The Direct Experience Network

Each person's brain uses two distinct and opposite pathways to interact with the world: the *default network* and the *direct experience network*. The default network is responsible for planning, daydreaming, ruminating, and directing your attention to a mental narrative about what's going on rather than to your direct experience. It's the network that is at the ready during most of your waking moments, turning on when not much else is happening.

Let's say you're taking a leisurely walk on a beautiful day with the sun shining and the breeze blowing gently. With the default network engaged, instead of experiencing the sun or the breeze, you're thinking about what to cook for dinner. One thought leads to another, and soon your mind is on grocery shopping, your activities for the rest of the week, and on and on. When the default network is dominant, you don't experience much about your actual walk.

But there's another way to go for a walk, one in which you experience beginner's mind and the brain's other pathway, the direct experience network, is dominant. The direct experience network keeps you engaged in the moment—free from labels, judgments, expectations, assumptions, or any other digressions of the mind into the past or future. Your awareness meets your experience directly and is absorbed by your senses in real time. You can tap into this other network by shifting your focus to the present moment through breath or body awareness, as you learned to do in Week One; or take some long, slow, deep breaths as you learned in Week Two.

When you engage the mind's direct experience network, labels and ideas recede into the background, allowing what you actually experience to be in the forefront of your awareness. Your senses are enlivened without the obstructing overlay of those narrative thoughts. With your direct experience network, you are present in each moment of your walk. With your beginner's mind, you feel your body moving through space, warmed by the sun, and caressed by the gentle breeze. It is a sublime experience and completely nourishing.

Studies show that regular meditation practice can change regions of the brain associated with remembering, labeling, and narrating. A meditator's brain can more easily interrupt the connection between the default and direct experience networks, allowing for longer periods of direct experiences. Doing this week's exercises along with your daily meditation practice will help you stabilize the direct experience network and train your brain to let go of your know-it-all mind. You'll cultivate a nonjudgmental awareness of your experiences —the very basis of beginner's mind.

Beginner's Mind and Interconnectedness

There are trillions of atoms in each of us, so every time you breathe in there's a good chance you just inhaled atoms that circulated in your mother's lungs at the time of your birth. Take in a few more breaths. It's also possible you've breathed atoms that Martin Luther King, Jr., breathed when delivering his memorable speech, "I Have a Dream," or the atoms that Mother Teresa breathed as she did her compassionate work in Calcutta. Based on your breath containing about one liter of air, and calculating the atoms in that liter as compared to the atoms in the atmosphere overall through the ages (yes, there's actually a formula for this), it's not ridiculous to make such claims.

It may seem as if we live in a world of separate objects, with each person and thing having a unique individuality, existing in time, and with edges in space. But this sensory view could very well be an illusion, considering what we now know about matter at its most basic level. The domain of modern quantum physics shows that, in reality, matter (and thus our bodies) is a wave structure of the universe, vibrating and resonating with everything else in the space that exists in and around us. Subtly, we are all interconnected to everything in the universe. Not only is this modern science, it's also an enlightened perspective that mystics and sages through the ages have realized. Therefore, although we perceive our bodies as separate objects, we can also keep in mind that perception is just an illusion limited by our sensory apparatus.

We all want to belong, to be included, to feel connected with others—and we actually are. But when the mind is preoccupied with labels and the ideas of things, it tends to categorize, and thus separate us from what is actually before us. For example, whenever my husband attends a football game, he keeps his distance from the people wearing a different team's colors or logo on their shirts. Although he does it in the spirit of team loyalty, it illustrates how easy it is to label another person and create an "us versus them" mentality.

When you label something, you exclude it. In other words, when you see a tree and recognize it as an oak tree, you *know* what it is, you label it, and it's done. It's not a living being, it's not interconnected with everything else in the space. In fact, you don't truly see it anymore. The tree is perceived only in your own mind. In this way you can completely miss how the tree is interconnected with the wind that moves it, the sunlight that nourishes it, the space that is provided for it to grow, the rain that waters it, and the earth on which it stands rooted. You, yourself, are also part of the tree, when you look at it. Perhaps you're also taking in some of the oxygen this tree generates. Maybe you've never thought about a tree this way, but when you view things with a beginner's mind, you sense your connection with each and every part of nature, and the interconnection of all things becomes clear.

This point is exemplified in the story of Dr. Jill Bolte-Taylor, a Harvard-trained neuroanatomist who learned about the brain's workings and the perception of beginner's mind personally. She had a stroke at age 37, an experience she wrote about in her book, *My Stroke of Insight*. She describes how the mental chatter completely disappeared that morning of her stroke. Her brain's left hemisphere (an area that regulates ego and self-image, analysis, labels, judgment, and identifying separate parts) had been damaged and gone off-line.

With only her right hemisphere functioning (which is the area of the brain that regulates creativity, empathy, intuition, and synthesis), her perception changed radically. She didn't see her body as a composition of skin, arms, and legs; instead, she saw the atoms and molecules that composed her body as they blended with the space around her. She no longer could discern where her body ended and the outside world began; rather, everything seemed to be part of the "same magnificent field of shimmering energy." She felt euphoric.

Although Dr. Taylor's spirit was soaring, her body was struggling to live. She lost the ability to speak, to understand numbers or letters, and even to recognize her own mother. A friend took her to the hospital where she underwent surgery, and eight years of rehabilitation followed. She's recovered now and travels around the country talking about her experience, describing herself as one who "can step into the consciousness of my right hemisphere" on command and be "one with all that is."

We can share Dr. Taylor's insight and choose to live a more peaceful, spiritual life by sidestepping our dominant left brain and perceiving life more directly through our right brain. This is training for beginner's mind, and meditation is an excellent method to develop it.

Creativity and Beginner's Mind

A friend of mine, Jennifer, showed me some pictures she'd drawn of herself at a workshop based on the book *Drawing on the Right Side of the Brain* by Betty Edwards. The one done on the first day of the workshop was a funny-looking cartoonish face of a girl, not much different from what a ten-year-old might draw. But the self-portrait she'd drawn at the end of the workshop was amazingly accurate and well done. Jennifer's told me that her new creative ability stemmed from a shift in perception, a result of activating her right brain: moving from the know-it-all mind to the beginner's mind.

We all naturally know how to draw, but our habit of perception interferes with our ability. According to Betty Edwards, to draw well we need to perceive edges, spaces, relationships, lights, and shadows; we need to see the whole scene, or *gestalt*. One way Edwards suggests that you can learn to draw is by changing your perception. Let's say you're copying a picture. When your mind begins to label familiar things in the picture you are copying, it can get in the way of seeing clearly, and this makes it more difficult to draw. She suggests that by simply turning the image upside down, your mind can't as easily label familiar things. So instead of labels, your mind focuses on the lines, shadows, edges, and spaces that you perceive. This refocusing tones down the left brain's activity of labeling and separating what you see so you can draw what is actually there. Eventually, the right side of the brain takes over, and your state of consciousness shifts.

Activating the right-brain mode to change your state of consciousness has a lasting, pleasurable effect. You become more alert, relaxed, confident, clear headed, interested, and absorbed by what you are doing, unaware of the passage of time. You notice a profound connection between you and what you're doing—a sense of oneness, often accompanied by calmness, exhilaration, and bliss. You can see why people continue their creative endeavors, meditate, or pray. It feels so good!

A Meditator's Story: Letting Go of Judgment

Judith, a mother and entrepreneur from Tucson, Arizona, was already a seasoned meditator before she came to me to deepen her practice. She was undergoing a period of extreme stress and was about to dissolve her marriage of 20 years.

She confided to me, "After coming from very little financial resources and building a business empire on our own, my husband, Bill; our three children; and I lived in a mansion in a private gated community. Then it all fell away, and our family went from having $35 million in assets and income to declaring bankruptcy, living off of food stamps, and being pretty much homeless. At one point our difficulties made it obvious that we were disconnected as a couple. Bill continued to work his tail off trying to make money, but emotionally and mentally, he was unbearable to live with."

After Judith recommitted to her meditation practice to relieve the stress, she found an unexpected side benefit: she was able to "soften her opinion" of her husband and of life in general, letting go of judgments and seeing life with a beginner's mind.

One day, she had a moment of complete clarity after her meditation, and all her judgments fell away. As she told me, "In my mind's eye, I saw Bill's face, the face of the man I met in college. I saw him in his football uniform leading his team to a championship. I remembered his competitive nature and his desire to win. Then I saw him at his first job. His persistence and honesty made him the best salesman in a major corporation, and he became the youngest vice president in the company.

"His passion for saving people's lives flooded into my consciousness next: as the youngest certified paramedic in the country at only 15 years old, he had risked his life to save people who'd fallen into frozen lakes outside of Chicago, rescued residents from burning buildings, dragged others out of crashed cars, and wrestled an overdosing heroin addict to the ground to give him a lifesaving injection. Then I saw Bill after the birth of all three of our babies . . . those same strong arms and hands holding them, protecting them. Protecting *me*.

"This thought came: *What would happen if I stopped judging him and just let him be who he is?* A few hours after I had this thought, I returned home after a long day. I expected things to be the same between Bill and me—we were set on getting a divorce as soon as we could afford to live apart. I walked into our dining room to find him sitting at the table with our wedding candle in front of him, the flame burning as it had on the day we were married. He'd also had a realization. He told me he needed to work through his issues and asked me to give him time to do so. Because I'd been meditating, I was no longer judging him and open to all possibilities. So I agreed to his request."

Recently the couple met with a psychologist and shared their story. The therapist told them that in 35 years of practice, she'd never seen a couple handle obstacles as well as they did. She wanted to know their secret.

Judith told her, "For me, the secret lies in the magic of meditation. I've learned to let go of judgments of people and the world. The results may not be as obvious as when it saved my marriage— mostly they're subtle. But the magic is always waiting for me whenever I need it."

Practices and Exercises to Cultivate Freedom

Three Beginner's Mind Moments

There are many ways to cultivate a beginner's-mind perspective. Here are three suggestions compiled from my own experience and the experiences of my students:

— Go out to dinner at your favorite restaurant. When the waiter comes for your order, say that you'd like the chef to make you whatever he or she wants. Then, when the food comes to your table, savor it fully, enjoying the surprise that comes with having no expectations. I did this recently and experienced the best meal I'd ever had! I also met the chef, who was excited to serve something new.

— Choose a day during which you accept whatever anyone offers to you. (Make it a few days if you like.) Say yes when you ordinarily might say no out of habit. If someone invites you somewhere, say yes. Whatever food is offered to you, accept it gratefully. If someone asks you to do something, say yes. Keep a childlike awareness, free from expectations. You never know where it will lead you.

— At a movie theater, or on your own TV, view a nonviolent movie you know nothing about. As you watch, notice how your narrative mind might want to judge it one way or another, even as being good or bad. When you notice the labels or judgment, bring your attention back to your direct experience. Enjoy the movie as it unfolds, and simply experience it and yourself as you watch.

Delectable Eating

This exercise is one of my favorites to cultivate a beginner's mind. People are often surprised by their experience, which is exactly why I love to do it! You can do this exercise alone or with friends or family (kids love this!). Maintain an inner focus and do the practice in silence. It should take about 15 minutes. To get started, all you need is a piece of ripe fruit.

Here's what to do:

— Create a quiet environment. Turn off electronic devices and other sources of noise. Sit quietly and comfortably as if you were getting ready for a sitting meditation.

— Place a piece of fruit in front of you on a plate or napkin.

— Close your eyes. Allow yourself several slow, long, deep breaths through your nose.

— Let your breath return to its natural rhythm. Bring your attention to the sensation of your breath for a minute or two.

— Let your awareness come to the present moment. What do you hear? What do you smell? How are you feeling? Scan your body, relaxing and releasing tension from your muscles. Notice how you are supported as you sit.

— Pay attention to what emotions are present. Allow yourself to feel them as they arise.

— When you feel relaxed and present, open your eyes softly and look at the fruit. Avoid labeling or naming anything you experience from this moment on. Simply enjoy what you feel, smell, taste, touch, and hear as you experience this exercise.

— Slowly pick up the fruit. Turn it in your hand, and notice how it feels, taking into consideration the weight, temperature, and texture. No naming; instead, simply feel and sense.

— As you examine it, notice something about this type of fruit you have never noticed before. Pay close attention to the shape, color, and texture. See the light reflect off its surface. Avoid naming any of the attributes. Simply see. (If it is an orange or banana and needs to be peeled, now is the time to do that. Take your time doing so; notice the peel separating from the fruit, along with the textures and temperatures and smells of each.)

— Now close your eyes and bring the fruit under your nose. Notice if there is a smell that meets your awareness, but don't name it. Simply smell it.

— Rub the fruit over your closed lips. Focus on the sensations.

— Take a small bite out of it and chew it slowly and deliberately, resisting the urge to swallow. As you chew, notice the immediate change in the intensity of the flavor. Listen to its sound as you chew. No labels—just tasting, listening.

— Keep it in your mouth as long as you can before you swallow. Notice any feeling or urge to change the experience.

— If thoughts come up, gently return your attention to the experience at hand. Fully appreciate the pleasures of seeing, smelling, touching, listening, and tasting.

— Breathe in deeply again after you finish the first bite. Continue to relax.

— Again, look at the fruit and notice any differences in the texture, color, shape, and smell from where you took the bite.

— Give yourself another bite and follow the same procedure. Avoid labels, judgments, assumptions, and ideas of what should happen. Be fully present for this experience. Do it slowly. Keep breathing.

— When you feel complete, sit quietly with your eyes closed until you feel that it's time to move back into everyday activity.

— Keep this newness of the experience with you and see if you can apply the same principles to other activities throughout your day.

Walking Without Labels

This practice is designed to create a new way of experiencing the world. As you walk, let whatever you see, smell, taste, touch, and hear meet your awareness, without labeling or identifying anything. Do this exercise with your eyes open all the way, focusing on nothing in particular; or with capped eyes, gazing softly toward the ground about three to four feet in front of you. I like to do this practice outside but it can be done anytime and anywhere.

— Start by standing where you are, giving attention to your breath and your body for a moment. Relax while feeling the support of your breath, your body, and the earth.

— Begin walking. You can do this exercise slowly or moving at a normal pace. However you move, keep refocusing your attention on the moment at hand.

— As you walk, connect with the essence of whatever you encounter: listen, look, touch, and smell (taste, too, if that's appropriate) as if you were experiencing it for the first time. Resist the urge to label anything that meets your eyes or ears, whether it's a bird, tree, car, or cloud.

— Explore what you experience with curiosity and openness.

— Avoid categorizing or preferring one thing over another. If you notice yourself doing so, return to your beginner's mind, simply sensing each object of your experience and the qualities of it. Notice shapes, edges, light, reflections, shadows, colors, movement, density, sound, texture, and other qualities.

— Whenever you notice your attention drifting away, come back to the present moment by becoming aware of your body and breath and movements. Then return to the exercise.

— Continue to walk this way for five to ten minutes.

Schedule of Practices and Exercises

Week Three: Suggested Daily Practices	
AM	Long, Slow, Deep Breathing: 3 Minutes Sitting Meditation: 12 Minutes
PM	Walking Without Labels: 3 Minutes Sitting Meditation:12 Minutes

Additional Awareness Exercises	
Anytime	Delectable Eating Body Awareness Three Beginner's Mind Moments

Insights for Success

Continue with your *Sitting Meditation* this week for 30 minutes a day. Practice *Walking Without Labels* and experience the *Delectable Eating* exercise to cultivate your beginner's mind. Remember to approach each meditation with innocence, letting go of any comparison to other meditation experiences you've had or heard about, or judgments about how it should go.

Eventually, your beginner's mind will extend to the rest of your life as your habitual attachment to assumptions and labels is loosened and you are relieved of the ideas that stand between you and experiencing the world as it truly is. You may find your experience of life goes beyond anything you ever imagined, where nothing is completely certain, and all possibilities are available. That's true freedom! Beginner's mind is often found to be one of the most rewarding and satisfying benefits on the meditation path and is an essential element of being soul-centered.

○ ○ ○

WEEK FOUR

COMPASSION: LOVE YOURSELF

"Love yourself first and everything falls into line."

— LUCILLE BALL, ACTRESS AND COMEDIENNE

You've been practicing mindfulness, sitting meditations, and awareness exercises for three weeks now . . . *congratulations!*

Maybe by this time your practice is becoming a habit. Meditation periods are probably easier to fit into your schedule. You may also be feeling calmer, with a heightened sense of self-awareness and more presence, both in and out of meditation. Perhaps you're experiencing the beginner's mind, meeting life with more clarity and freedom from judgments and assumptions. If you've yet to experience these effects, hang in there—don't give up. And through it all, be kind to yourself. Remember, 30 minutes of meditation each day for eight weeks can alter the actual physical structure of your brain, and that will definitely create some lasting changes you will be able to see.

This week's focus is on loving yourself. You will learn a *Loving Your Body* exercise to help transform your relationship with your body. You will also discover that it's okay not to believe all of your own thoughts. You've been practicing being kind to yourself while in meditation, but this week you will learn a specific *Loving*

Kindness Meditation to cultivate compassion for yourself and others equally. You'll find that by loving yourself, it becomes easier to love others, as well as let others love you.

Learning to Love Yourself

As a kid, I learned the Biblical commandment, *Love your neighbor as yourself.* I believed it was important to love others, and believed in the Golden Rule: *Do unto others as you would have them do unto you.* I practiced being kind to others, but I didn't realize the importance of loving myself or what that even entailed. Love thy neighbor *as thyself.* I didn't love them as I loved myself; I seemed to love them more.

Being kind to yourself, taking care of yourself, and loving yourself don't always come naturally. It's something you learn from your family, culture, and community. I didn't learn it from mine and maybe you didn't from yours either, but it's never too late to start. Many resist the concept of putting themselves first, because they were raised to do the opposite—to put others first and themselves last. Flight attendants always give the warning: during an emergency, you must first put on your own oxygen mask before trying to help others with theirs. It's a good reminder that you can't aid others until you take care of yourself first. It took me years to apply this simple rule to my own life.

One person who knows about self-love and self-care is my friend Kathy. We've been co-leaders for retreats for years. She's a dedicated spiritual teacher and inspirational singer and songwriter, and I truly don't know of any woman who takes better care of herself. When we travel together, Kathy easily asks for help carrying her suitcases and unloading her sound equipment. She sets up her hotel room like it's a sacred space, with all her favorite foods, including organic fruits and nuts, and her preferred coffee and creamer. She carefully unpacks her dry-cleaned clothes and hangs them up perfectly. She makes sure to get enough exercise and aims to get plenty of sleep. In the morning she spreads her bath towel on the floor and does yoga, then lovingly fixes her hair and applies her body lotion. She is particular about what she eats and is careful about the environments she's in, being sure that nothing is too toxic. All this, while she's on the road!

My style is a little different. I'm more likely to arrive at a destination with only a stash of airplane peanuts in my purse for a snack, praying that my clothes aren't too wrinkly as I quietly lug my overstuffed suitcase. I may have forgotten my body lotion, but I really don't notice. I'm quick about fixing my hair, throwing in a clip. Somehow, in spite of my more spontaneous style, I'm good to go. But when I watch Kathy lovingly care for herself, I realize my own self-care could be better. It's all relative, of course. We are both dedicated to service, but Kathy is a shining example of how to take good care of yourself without guilt or apology, while still serving others generously.

Becoming aware of how you care—or don't care—for your body, mind, and soul is the first step on the path to self-love. Meditation is key to help you be more aware and see things more clearly. With awareness, you notice your internal monologue and when you say disparaging things about yourself. With meditation and the intention to adopt a kinder, authentic, more loving, compassionate attitude toward yourself, you can transform.

The Science of Loving Yourself

While meditation has long been known for calming the mind, improving focus, and increasing contentment, researchers have recently proved that meditation can also foster compassion. It turns out that the areas of the brain related to empathy and compassion are more active in those who meditate than in those who don't. And now there's a new area of research known as self-compassion, which is a compassionate attitude toward oneself.

Self-compassion is related to curiosity and exploration, and is made up of three components. The first is "self-kindness," being kind and understanding toward yourself rather than critical. The second is "common humanity," which means accepting your tough times as being a normal part of being human. The third component is "mindful acceptance," which means remaining peaceful when painful thoughts and feelings arise, rather than overidentifying with them.

In 2007, Duke University researchers discovered that treating yourself with compassion increases your well-being and helps eliminate much of the anger, depression, and pain that people experience during unpleasant life events. They found that self-compassion includes the ability to be self-aware, insightful, and see reality as it is. They suggested that some of the benefits usually associated with self-esteem are in fact due to self-compassion.

Self-compassion is different from self-esteem. Self-esteem is associated with how highly people regard themselves for achievements, talents, or social rank, as well as how special they think they are. Self-esteem has not been proven to support emotional calmness in the midst of distress, but self-compassion has. This is because self-compassion reduces feelings of being threatened, insecure, and defensive. Self-compassion enhances our ability to comfort ourselves emotionally, and this helps us feel safer and more secure. Numerous studies show how self-compassion helps reduce stress linked to depression and other illnesses.

Research also shows that self-compassionate people take full responsibility for their actions, good or bad. They maintain perspective, recovering and regaining equilibrium from upsets more quickly without feeling the need to add an extra layer of catastrophe. This goes against the philosophy behind the practice of being hard on yourself as a way to instill discipline or correct your own behavior. You may have noticed that negative thinking is defeating rather than motivating, but it could be that you didn't know any alternatives to being tough on yourself.

You can rest assured that self-compassion is more motivating and effective than any negative motivating methods are. It's even been proven to be an effective motivator for weight loss. Consider one study in which researchers at Wake Forest University in North Carolina asked female college students to take part in what they called a food-tasting experiment. Two groups of women were asked to eat a doughnut (which the researchers chose because doughnuts are commonly viewed as a "forbidden" or "guilty" food). One group was given a short speech in self-compassion at the beginning of the experiment, urging the women not to feel guilty since all the particapants were eating doughnuts, too. The other group wasn't given that lesson. The women were then given candy to taste-test while they filled out a questionnaire. Researchers found that the women who were given the lesson in self-compassion were less distressed and ate less candy than those in the control group.

You may resist being nice to yourself because you feel it's selfish. You might be afraid you'll become self-indulgent or self-absorbed. No one wants to be viewed in such a way. But consider this: self-compassion could be the missing ingredient in successfully reaching your goals such as weight-loss and other endeavors in which you usually tell yourself to "suck it up" or "tough it out." So instead of being hard on yourself, feeling guilty, or depriving yourself, consider cultivating self-compassion to more easily shift into healthier behaviors.

Loving Yourself in Meditation—and in Life

Your internal thought process can be less than kind during your meditation practice, especially when you think you're not having the "perfect" meditation. (Believe me, I know how you feel.) Self-critical thoughts such as *I can't do this, This isn't working,* or *What's wrong with me?* are common. Even though you've been instructed to welcome whatever happens, it can be discouraging to not be able to stop your mind from wandering. *I just have to try harder,* you say to yourself—then you remember that trying hard in meditation doesn't help. In jumps the next, defeating thought, *I can't ever do it right,* and you immediately feel that there is something wrong with you. When this happens, people often give up meditation altogether. But you don't have to do that. Everyone gets distracted or daydreams at times, but that's no reason to let your thoughts take you on a ride. As I often remind my students, truly anyone can meditate.

If you have a hard-on-yourself attitude in meditation, then it is most likely that this self-critical voice follows you through your day, too. This voice feeds you one-liners, like *I'm too fat, Everyone else knows more than me, I'm not lovable—I hope no one will find out, I'm not as good as her/him,* and *I don't deserve it anyway.* By addressing these thoughts in meditation, you learn to be kind to yourself at all times, and not just when you're meditating. A compassionate attitude toward yourself is not only a fundamental element to a successful meditation practice, it is also essential for a soul-centered life.

There's plenty of advice on how to cultivate self-compassion and self-love, including journaling, getting regular massages, eating well, getting enough sleep, exercising, relaxing, getting out into nature, singing, listening to music, using aromatherapy, cleaning out your closets, reading a good book, saying affirmations, and taking a hot bath. These are all great suggestions, and most of us know about them. So why are we still so hard on ourselves? It's simply a habit, and it isn't helpful.

Actions that support not loving yourself can become habitual simply because they've never been challenged. There are many ways that this often plays out. You could be staying in a relationship that isn't nourishing, or saying nasty things to yourself when you look in the mirror. Perhaps you don't take good care of your body, or you don't listen to your own inner wisdom. Research shows that those who are considered kind and helpful to others score surprisingly low on questionnaires involving self-compassion.

So let's get back to loving thy neighbor as thyself. If you're in the habit of not treating yourself well, and you "love your neighbor as yourself," then maybe you sometimes treat your neighbor (or co-worker or family member) in the same unkind way that you treat yourself. You might think some unpleasant things about him or her or be uncaring in other ways. You see how that goes?

To cultivate self-compassion, you have to pay attention to yourself, like you'd expect a good friend to pay attention to you. Maybe you've forgotten your own inner beauty or sweetness. Be open and get to know yourself as you've been doing since the first week of this program. When you truly pay attention to yourself, you realize that you are not your self-image—the labels you call yourself, the roles you take on, the work you do, the responsibilities you have, or your weight or age. Instead, you are more than that. You are a compassionate, wise, kind, aware, and peaceful being.

You learn new ways to be kinder to yourself throughout this program; and this week, you learn to love your body, be present with your own pain, question thoughts that make you unhappy, and say nice things to yourself. When you're kind to yourself, it becomes much easier to be kind to your neighbor. With compassion and self-compassion is how a soul-centered life is lived.

Learning to Love My Body

In 1993, I was diagnosed with thyroid cancer. I had moved to San Diego to work at the Sharp Institute for Mind-Body Medicine, and with my new job came health insurance. I chose an endocrinologist as my primary-care physician, and when I met with her for the first time, she palpated my thyroid gland. "There's a lump there—let's aspirate it," she said, and biopsied my thyroid with a very long needle. I wasn't surprised because I'd noticed this lump a few years earlier. My throat often ached, especially when I was sad, upset, or held down my emotions (which I usually did).

Two days later, she called me with the news that I had papillary carcinoma—cancer. Before that phone call, I knew myself as a healthy woman. When I heard the news, I expected to suddenly feel sick or injured, but no feelings came—except a vague sense of emptiness and a little tingling of fear. Later, I felt guilty: *How could I work at a mind-body health center and have cancer? I must've done something wrong.* In the beginning of the alternative-health movement, there were people saying that a person with a disease must have done something to cause it. Although none of my co-workers nor the Ayurvedic texts I read supported this viewpoint, there were still plenty of sick people blaming themselves for their disease—and now I was one of them. This was not helpful.

I sought out Deepak Chopra's advice, since he too was an endocrinologist by training. Because of his fame, many people called and sent letters with their medical records, pleading for an appointment with him. Since I worked for him and felt he was my friend, I couldn't help but think, *I'm one of the lucky ones.* I desperately wanted him to give me a *mantra*, a special sound I could use in my meditation, a magic bullet that would heal me or pave the way for a spontaneous remission.

He gave me a mantra in the ancient language of Sanskrit, which I was to use silently, then added: "But you should also get that tumor removed." Yes, there was a possibility of a spontaneous healing, he told me, but such events are rare no matter what mantra, treatment, herbs, crystals, intentions, good thoughts, or diet anyone followed. "A person's physiology can be slow to respond to their shifts in awareness, so you should get the surgery soon," he advised.

President Clinton had just passed the Family and Medical Leave Act that allowed anyone with a serious health condition to take a leave of absence from his or her job, so I went on my own version of a vision quest. I decided to pursue some additional alternative treatments before having surgery. *Who knows,* I thought, *maybe I'll be one of those rare people who spontaneously heals.* Not only did I meditate and use my new healing mantra, I got crystal healings, took herbs, and had Reiki treatments. Prayers were said across the country for me.

I also read up on what this cancer represented energetically. It may have been obvious to some, but to me it wasn't. The throat represents communication with others and with ourselves. A thyroid problem can be seen as a metaphor for "not having a voice." It represents a blockage in the junction point between the heart and the head and the inability to hear our own wisdom, express our emotions, and express ourselves in the world. Early in life,

I learned to swallow my tears and anger, not express my truth, and to be focused on the needs of others. I held back my emotions in exchange for being loved and accepted. Due to a long-term hearing loss, my father was so irritated by children's voices that he would react with rage the moment he heard a child cry or speak loudly—including one of his own. I imagine that because of this, I made the decision early in life not to speak up or speak my truth. (Perhaps that's why I had regular bouts with strep throat and extreme coughing fits throughout my childhood.) Once that junction between heart and head is open, feeling and expressing emotions is easy, whether negative or positive. You can speak up for yourself and ask for what you want.

I now knew what the problem was, but I wasn't fluent in feeling my emotions or in expressing my truth . . . so I looked for more ways to heal. One approach I used was a then-popular visualization technique, imagining the cancer cells as an enemy to be conquered in battle. One night, I realized that imagining a war within my body was causing me more stress, not less. So I tried something new: I turned my practice of battling the cancer into a practice of loving my body. I felt love and acceptance even toward the cancerous cells in my throat area. I felt compassion for them and their misguided programming that caused them to grow in such a malignant way. As I stayed focused on embracing rather than battling my cancer, a wave of peace arose from deep inside me and washed over my entire body.

While I still needed to use conventional treatments, this new practice marked a turning point in my life. A few days before Christmas, I had the surgery. Before surgery, in my hospital room with the lights turned down low, I lit incense (even though the nurses rushed in and asked me to put it out) and meditated. As I was being wheeled into the surgery suite, I asked my Harvard-trained vascular surgeon to listen to soothing music while operating and say only positive things. I figured it couldn't hurt.

Your body overhears everything. Words have a vibration that carries their meaning, and your body listens to all you say or think (and what others say to you or about you). Observe your words as you describe your body to yourself or others. Consider the story a friend told me about a young mother she sat next to on a plane. The woman had her thyroid gland removed due to Hashimoto's disease, an autoimmune disorder. Her doctor warned that her ovaries were next to go, because, he said, "Your body is killing you."

This woman was suffering, not only from the disease, but from the belief she'd been encouraged to adopt about her own body—that "it" was killing her, as if her body were the enemy. I'm sure you've heard people say "I have a bad back" or "That's my bad knee." But is their knee or back really bad? Injured perhaps, sore perhaps, diseased, perhaps. But *bad?* I doubt it. It's important to watch how you talk to yourself or believe what others say about you. Remember, your body is constantly listening to the dialogue going on in your mind and responds in kind.

It's been proven over and over again that when you are at peace, your immune system is enhanced and healing is easier. I was at peace, and I recovered quickly from my surgery, which was successful in removing the tumor. I had more work to do, which I'll share with you in the upcoming weeks. I've not had a recurrence of the cancer, and I continue to this day to practice loving my body. Fortunately, you don't have to have cancer to learn to love your body. You can love it right now by giving your body loving attention. You can do it anytime, anywhere with your awareness, in or out of meditation.

I hope you find inspiration in the following story of how one of my students learned to love herself and put her cancer into remission.

A Meditator's Story: I've Learned to Love Myself

Monica was diagnosed with cancer in her 20s. The doctors she worked with recommended that she learn to meditate as part of her healing process. This was the first time she'd heard about meditation, but she came to a weekend meditation retreat I was leading in Sedona and began meditating on a daily basis.

"When I first learned to meditate," she later told me, "I realized that there was a connection with something greater than myself—a free flow of source energy. It became an opportunity for exploration and opened up a whole new world for me. I was able to move beyond my self-imposed limitations and started asking the questions about what my heart truly wanted. I could see more clearly what I wanted to do in life and how I was going to get there."

Her meditation experience prompted Monica to get certified in Reiki and life coaching, learning as much as she could to heal herself and others. Trained as a social worker, she had planned to get a master's degree in counseling; but as she progressed toward her goal, she realized that she wanted to learn about how the body and emotions are involved in healing, and it was more than she could get from a counseling degree. She began working with several holistic healers, changed her diet, continued her meditation practice, and visualized herself being healthy.

In eight months, the cancer was completely gone without her having to undergo any radiation, chemotherapy, or surgery. That was six years ago. Today, she's still in remission. Monica lives in Hawaii and studies acupuncture and Chinese medicine. She is currently interning to complete her master's program and will be licensed in one more year.

Monica credits this complete transformation of her life to her meditation practice. "Before I began meditating, I was severely depressed for years. I struggled with an overwhelming sense of sadness and felt like there was something more I was supposed to be doing but didn't know how to move forward. I felt stagnant.

"Meditation supports the realization that you are a perfect being. We are all perfect, and the body wants to naturally align with that truth. We forget about our wholeness, and meditation pulls us back into that feeling of completion and perfection."

When people who knew Monica before see her now, they often remark that she seems so much calmer and happier. Even her own sister notices the difference and has told her when she visits, "I just love having you around, because you bring such a peaceful energy to my life when you're here."

Monica's relationship with herself transformed too. She says, "I've learned to love myself for where I already am, not being so concerned about where I'm going to get to. If there's something I want to feel, like fulfillment or happiness, I can feel that immediately—I don't have to wait. I can enjoy the process and accept myself for what's going on right now. My depression from my younger days stemmed from always looking for outside sources to fulfill me. The reality is, we have everything we need inside of us, and meditating brought me to that understanding."

She also saw a shift in her romantic relationships. "I started noticing patterns in my relationships. I could be perfectly fine and independent on my own, but as soon as I got into a relationship, I would automatically defer to the other person for my happiness. Putting all that pressure and expectations on another person led to my relationships deteriorating. When I started meditating, I started to understand my own happiness, and it changed the way I related to people.

"Meditation has changed so much in my life. Now, if I have negative experiences, I take it as a sign to check in with myself and ask: 'How am I attracting this?' Such experiences mean it's time to get back to center, to loving myself. This awareness dramatically changes how I interact with people on a daily basis, letting me feel more independent and confident."

Feel to Heal

If a family member, friend, or neighbor tells you that he or she is sick with the flu (or even something more serious), you naturally offer words of comfort. Maybe you bring flowers, spend time with that person, and cook some soup. If you heard a baby crying, you would probably move toward it, too, bringing your full attention to comfort or assuage the infant's distress—whether it's a colicky tummy ache or a wet diaper. Those kinds of responses are compassion in action.

When I found out I had cancer and told people in my life, it seemed to make them uncomfortable or even scare them in some way. I know from working in the healing field and seeing other people go through illness that friends and family often don't know how to respond. Instead of coming to be with the person who is ill, they stay away, perhaps feeling inadequate to help or not knowing what to say. This may be because they are not comfortable with their own pain.

Some of us want to avoid pain at all costs, even while it's happening. Imagine that you just stubbed your toe. It hurts, so you hop around the room trying to distract yourself from the pain. God knows, it could be broken, and you don't want to even look at it until the pain subsides. Just as an infant cries out when it wants to be comforted, your toe is crying out with pain.

You may have gotten into the habit of ignoring or struggling against your own pain or the pain of others. You may have forgotten how to love yourself or others. But with awareness, you can consciously approach illness, injury, and pain with love. It's natural. When you injure yourself, your hand instinctively grabs the injured area. Touch is the instinctive way we love and heal ourselves and others. Healing involves moving toward pain rather than away from it. Whether you touch a painful area with your hand, or keep a sick friend company with your loving presence, you are being compassionate.

You can make a conscious choice to be present for the pain and create a new habit. Exercises such as Week One's *Body Awareness* help develop the ability to be present with your own pain and discomfort, which are very real parts of life. When you're intimate with your own pain, you're then able to be present with the pain of others. This is true for both physical and emotional pain. Instead of ignoring it, struggling against it, or distracting yourself or someone else from it, you embrace what *is*. Your loving attention to anything—whether it's your pain or someone else's, emotional or physical—is kindness in action. Often, there's nothing you need to say or do—simply being present with them is enough. Your loving presence is your gift and helps bring about healing in yourself and in the other.

Theories from quantum physics support this, asserting that any situation can change simply by your being present and bearing witness to it. When you observe a situation impartially, your observation can change it. In other words, it's impossible to observe something without its being impacted by your interaction with it. This happens not only on a subatomic level, but also in everyday life. When you observe your pain or the pain of another, when you are truly and fully present for it, that pain can be transformed.

My Journey to Self-Love

If you find yourself time and again in relationships that make you feel unlovable, then you're probably short on self-love. I had relationships like this, endless emotional loops of feeling bad about myself and looking to a partner to make me feel good. It was classic co-dependence and a very unstable way to be. Wanting love from someone else led me to do crazy things like elope with a man I'd casually met on the beach in south Florida.

I was 19 when we got married and on Christmas leave from basic training. My new husband was in his mid-20s, and his free spirit excited me. But he turned out to be more than free-spirited. He used drugs, had a long arrest record, and was violent toward me. In the beginning, he wasn't so bad, but fairly soon he threatened my life—and proceeded to do it again and again.

At that age, I felt basically unlovable. I didn't know I could be treated any other way than the way my new husband was treating me, and I even thought I deserved it on some level. One day, about a year into the so-called marriage, I knew I had to escape. I finally realized that I didn't want to live life like that. I don't know what caused such a shift in me . . . maybe it was grace. I am still grateful for it. In preparing to leave, I secretly applied to college, and left him as soon as I got accepted.

By the time I was in my mid-30s, I'd been meditating for a while. Although I had developed some self-awareness, I still had serious blind spots when it came to being in a healthy relationship—this was made very clear by the relationship I was in. I was getting ready to move from the Zen Center when I met a man we'll call Chris, and felt an immediate attraction to him. We had lots in common, too: we were both into meditation, yoga, cooking, and dance. We dated briefly before I moved to the tiny town of Mount Shasta in Northern California to work.

After a few weeks, Chris joined me. We shared a small cottage near the center of town. A few months into the relationship, he seemed to lose interest in me physically, which triggered my sense of low self-worth. His comments echoed the words of my ex-husband from years ago, "You're fat and ugly." I stayed in the relationship, hoping he would change his mind and grow to love me again, because I thought that's what I needed to feel good about myself.

We decided to visit the Zen Center where we met in order to attend a meditation retreat to welcome the new year. A day or two into it, during one of the meditation periods, I sneaked a peek at Chris who was sitting to the left of me. He wasn't sitting with capped eyes gazing at the floor in front of him; instead, he was staring across the room at an attractive woman who had arrived the day before. I felt furious, and instead of taking the emotional bypass I used to rely upon (pretending "it's all good"), I got real. I made a decision right then and there to take care of myself and to leave the retreat as soon as the final bell rang. To stay there wasn't in my integrity. Getting out of there *was*. I called a friend who was heading off to a juice fast in Malibu, and as quickly as I could pack a bag, I was out the zendo door and on my way to join her.

Questioning My Beliefs

The juice fast turned out to be something called "The New Year's Mental Cleanse," run by a woman I hadn't met before, Byron Katie. Her inquiry work (known as "The Work") had become well known among my friends, but I had never experienced it. The weekend was designed to address physical and mental toxicity—just what I needed. We arrived while Katie (that's what people call her) was onstage discussing how to examine your thoughts through an inquiry process. I had the distinct sense that I was in the right place and could learn more from her about my mind than I would suffering in silence in the zendo.

"Suffering begins with a painful thought," Katie said, addressing the group. "We believe the thought we have before we even ask ourselves if it is true." When we believe such painful thoughts, they can lead to all kinds of feelings and behaviors that aren't nourishing. As a result, we suffer. During the program, I realized that she was right—this was exactly what was happening to me.

At the first break, I went to sit outside the room feeling really sad. When my friend asked how I was doing, I told her I wanted Chris to love me, that he *should* love me. Following the steps of the inquiry process we had just learned in the workshop, she asked me, "Is it true that Chris should love you?"

I answered yes, of course. Then she asked me whether I could *absolutely know* that it was true. I answered no, I couldn't know that he should love me, but I really wanted him to. She then asked how it made me feel when I believed that Chris should love me. I described my sadness and the sick feeling in my stomach; then I began to cry. I told her that when I believed that Chris should love me, I didn't feel love for myself at all. I felt unworthy and uncomfortable being around others, as if something were wrong with me. I felt fat and ugly, I didn't want to take care of myself, and I had no passion for life. I felt like the relationship wasn't working, and I'd never be in a good relationship. I finally blurted out, "That's when I say fuck it! I get so mad at Chris and don't trust him one bit. I don't love him at all, or anyone for that matter."

My friend lovingly waited a moment and then continued with the inquiry. "Who would you be without the thought?"

I closed my eyes. I imagined living my life without the thought, *Chris should love me.* After a moment, a deep shift happened. I felt a sense of relief, freer, more spacious.

"Without that thought I am free to be me without him. Without that thought I feel good about myself, authentic, and self-sufficient. Without that thought I love myself. It feels much, much better," I told her. *Instead of believing that Chris should love me,* I realized, *I should love me.* I had wanted Chris to do for me what I couldn't or hadn't done for myself. After this simple yet startling discovery, I still continued to live with him for a few more months, but began to accept that I didn't need him in order to love myself. I soon stopped believing my thoughts about Chris.

I continued to attend Katie's weekend retreats when I had time off, and soon I was hired to work for her. I gave my notice, packed up, and took off, driving from Mt. Shasta to Los Angeles. I drove through a January snowstorm in my old Volvo, studded snow tires and all. Los Angeles was a city I often said I'd never live in, but I'd cultivated enough of a beginner's mind to let go of preconceived ideas of it. I found the perfect house to live in near the beach and practiced my meditation morning and evening. The thoughts that had kept me trapped and unhappy most of my life were becoming less believable. I inquired into them as they arose, using what I learned from The Work, asking myself if I was certain that they were true.

A few months had passed since I'd broken up with Chris, and I realized that much of the heartache I was feeling was grief over how poorly I had treated myself. In every relationship I'd been in, I thought someone else should love me. I reminded myself that no one could love me if I couldn't love myself. It was clear: to find love, I had to fall in love with myself first.

I asked myself: *What would I do and how would I feel if I were in love?* I decided I would no longer wait for the perfect relationship; instead, I treated myself as I wanted others to treat me. The Golden Rule in reverse! I began to feel more compassion for myself than I'd ever felt before, more confidence, and more wholeness. My reference point had shifted from depending on others for my sense of self-worth, to being centered on my own soul, my own beautiful self.

It has certainly turned out to be a far more loving, stable way to live.

Affirmations for Self-Love

Some students ask me if affirmations for self-love work. I always say to give them a try. If nothing else, they make you more aware of how you feel about yourself. I invite you to do one now: what happens when you say to yourself, "I love and approve of myself" or "I am a sweet and beautiful being"? Say it again. Affirmations are an exploration. Notice if a doubting inner voice jumps right in to oppose what you have said.

Louise Hay, one of the first women to speak about the power of affirmations, has said, "When you begin to say an affirmation to yourself, all the negative messages come to the surface, and then you get to see what's in your way of loving yourself." With awareness you can consciously make a change. You can say affirmations as you look in the mirror into your own eyes and hear what arises. Saying affirmations sure beats the negative dialogue some of us automatically have with ourselves every time we see our own reflection.

I found a way to gently sneak affirmations around my critical inner voice: I do it when I listen to love songs. It began one day when I heard Billy Joel's "Just the Way You Are" on the radio. Love songs usually left me feeling bad because no one loved me;

but this time I decided to sing along. I felt silly at first, but I did it anyway, until it began to feel good.

When I first heard the song back in high school, I played it over and over again while holed up in my bedroom. But now as I sang along with the words, I changed the pronouns so that I could really feel like I was singing those words to myself. I was truly loving me, *just the way I am*. It made me realize how far I'd come from that desperate teenager who needed someone, anyone, to tell her they loved her just the way she was.

Practices and Exercises to Cultivate Compassion

Don't Believe Everything You Think

If a thought causes you stress, yet you can't break the habit of thinking it again and again, you can consciously decide to question the thought, rather than believe it right off the bat. The same goes for those thoughts people think about you. You don't have to believe them either. Instead of assuming that your thoughts are true, ask yourself these questions:

- *Who would I be if I didn't believe that thought?*
- *How would I live my life without the thought?*

Ask, then give yourself a moment to really feel into the answer. You may notice that when you ask yourself these questions, you experience a moment of peace and spaciousness. This is because your mind stops for a moment when the thought process is interrupted. Instead of staying on the level of thought activity, your awareness drops into the same silence that you experience in meditation, the same silence that underlies all your thoughts, the same silence of your soul. The fact that you can question yourself and your thoughts means there is a thinker of the thoughts, and that is who and what you connect to in this inquiry practice. This week, identify your thoughts that don't bring you happiness, and meet them with the questions above.

Loving Your Body

This exercise is similar to *Body Awareness* from Week One and includes being aware of and relaxing your body from head to toe, from front to back, from the inside out. But then, as you scan your body the second time around, do so with loving attention and gratitude for each area you come across. That quality of attending, or attention, can transform any relationship you may have toward your own body. As your body overhears your internal dialogue, it responds with changes in blood pressure, hormones, and even immune-system function. Your body is your best friend, and the place you call home. Treat yourself gently, don't try too hard, and stay with the practice. There is no right or wrong way to feel, even if you feel nothing. This week, do this practice before your sitting meditation for 5 to 15 minutes.

Here's how to do it:

— Sit in a comfortable position. Close your eyes and let your awareness turn inward.

— Pay attention to the natural rhythm of your breath, without trying to control or manipulate it. Take note of how you're feeling in the moment.

— Begin as you've done with the *Body Awareness* process. Gently scan your body while relaxing from head to toe.

— After you've scanned your body, go through the process again, this time with an attitude of gratitude. Acknowledge how your body supports you and serves you without asking anything from you.

— Feel appreciation for your body's ability to digest food, assimilate nourishment, and rid itself of toxicity. Appreciate your ability to see beauty, feel sweet caresses, listen to the sounds of nature, taste earthly delights, and smell enticing aromas. Appreciate your ever-present body and your heart, which has been beating 100,000 times a day since you were only a few cells in your mother's womb.

— Appreciate your body as your faithful servant. Your brain is at your command. Your lungs have drawn air for you since the day you were born; your bones give you support. Your feet let you stand up for yourself, your hands let you reach out toward others and take care of yourself. Your skin has served as a wise layer of protection. Your immune system is clear about what is on your side. Your cells replace themselves at the perfect time. Appreciate your body's intelligence as it aligns with the rhythms of nature, monitoring the movement of the moon, the planets, the stars, and the earth.

— Now, feel your body's subtle sensations from the inside. Bring your loving attention to each area of your body—feel into it and imagine that you're giving it a warm, loving embrace. You can move from head to toes or from toes to head. Feel into your limbs, your organs, your skeleton, your flesh. You might even be able to feel your heart beat.

— Experience the emotions and physical sensations as they arise.

— You might not feel as if you can be loving if you come across an area that's diseased, or a physical or emotional pain. Practice accepting your body exactly as it is. Do not reject any part of yourself or your body.

— If you start to wish that things were different or get into a story, refocus your attention to the sensation at hand and gently return to the attitude of loving appreciation.

— Toward the end of your practice, give yourself a few minutes to feel where your body begins and ends. Maybe the edges aren't so defined. Feel where the inside and the outside seem to be. Feel your vitality, your life force moving through every part of you, every cell in your body. Feel the energy enliven. This can be totally blissful when you connect to this glorious condition called *life*.

— When the period is over, keep your eyes closed for a minute or two more. Reflect on the wisdom your body communicates to you. You can even lie down.

Loving Kindness Meditation

The *Loving Kindness Meditation* is a simple, heart-centered meditation technique with its roots in Buddhism. It's practiced around the world to cultivate compassion for oneself and others. In this meditation practice, you gather your attention to focus on a specific phrase that you repeat silently. First, you direct that phrase and feeling of love toward someone you care about, then direct it toward yourself, then offer your well-wishing globally. You can do this meditation by itself, or before or after a period of the basic *Sitting Meditation.* This practice can take 10 to 20 minutes.

It's important to know that you don't have to force a particular feeling or get rid of unpleasant or undesirable ones in order to do this meditation. Do not expect to feel a particular way or judge and assess what you do feel. Take on the beginner's mind and allow whatever happens to just happen. If your mind wanders, notice what has captured your attention, then gently return to the practice at hand.

— To begin, choose a phrase or two that resonates with you from the list below or come up with a simple phrase of your own:

- *May you be well.*

- *May you be happy.*

- *May you be free from suffering.*

- *May you be free of pain and sorrow.*

- *May you be peaceful and at ease.*

- *May you feel loved.*

- *May you be surrounded by loving kindness.*

- *May you feel safe and cared for.*

- *May you find true happiness.*

— Be sure to have a clock or watch nearby so that you can keep track of time, or set a timer that you won't have to get up to turn off. Sit quietly and ready yourself for a silent meditation. Close your eyes or leave them capped. (Remember, capping is a practice of maintaining a soft unfocused gaze directed two to three feet in front of you.)

— Take three long, slow, deep breaths through your nose, then let your breath return to its natural rhythm.

— Scan your body, relaxing as you go. If you notice pain or tension in your body, guide your attention there, letting your attention be the love your body needs.

— When you feel settled and relaxed, shift your awareness to your heart center, gently placing your hand there if you like.

— Bring someone you care about into your awareness— a child, a parent, a partner, or anyone you feel love for or who has been good or inspiring to you. Get a feeling for his or her presence. Visualize this person or silently say his or her name. Silently and sincerely offer loving kindness using whatever phrases you've chosen. I like: *May you be happy, may you be free from suffering, may you know peace.*

— As you repeat the phrase silently, allow yourself to feel whatever emotions arise, whether it's love, sadness, bliss, or gratitude. There's no need to hurry and no need to force a feeling or make anything up. Keep your awareness in the present moment with the practice instead of going into a memory about them. Keep breathing naturally and continue to offer them loving kindness.

Be aware and present with whatever experience is happening, even if it feels like nothing at all.

— After three minutes or so, shift your attention inward, refocusing your attention on your heart. Continue to breathe naturally and notice the gentle rise and fall of your chest. Then, with the same sincerity, offer the same phrase of compassion to yourself.

— Give yourself time to feel whatever comes up. Perhaps you'll feel loving emotions, painful emotions, confusion regarding how you're feeling, or nothing at all. Whatever you feel is perfect, just as it is. You might feel physical sensations such as lightness, numbness, or physical pain. If pain comes up, don't ignore it, try to cover it up, pretend it's something else, or change it. Instead, bear witness to the actual sensation. Stay with the focus on yourself for three minutes or so, then come back to your heart center.

— Next, identify a neutral person, someone you may have met briefly—the bus driver, the supermarket cashier, or a delivery person. Even without knowing his (or her) name, get a sense of the person, imagining his face, or what he was doing when you encountered him. Offer the same phrases of compassion toward him that you offered toward your loved one and yourself. Bear witness to what you feel. After a few more minutes, come back to center, and scan your body to be sure you are still comfortable and relaxed.

— Next, identify someone with whom you are having difficulty. Imagine her (or him); get a feeling for her presence. Offer the same phrases of compassion to her. Notice if you have difficulty doing this practice, or come up with a judgment about her; if you do, refocus your awareness onto the area around your heart. Keep your attention in the present, wishing the person well. Imagine her well and happy. This may be challenging for you, but remember, it is a practice.

— Bear witness to what you're feeling, whether it's a pleasant, unpleasant, or numb sensation. Maintain a beginner's mind.

Even if this person hurt you in the past, you can't fully know her. Take your time. When you feel complete, relax your body and give yourself some deep breaths, focusing on your heart center. I have found that this practice shifts relationships, even if you don't feel much at all during it.

— Next, imagine those who you believe are suffering or in need. (You can practice this with any form of life, such as an animal or even an ecosystem.) Perhaps you are moved by accounts of the suffering that follows a natural or manmade disaster. Even if you don't know the specific people personally, think of others who are like you and have some of the same daily concerns as you do: parents, children, grandparents, business owners, animal lovers, and so on. Get a feeling for their presence. Keep them in your awareness and offer the same phrases of compassion to them: *May you be happy, may you be free from suffering, may you know peace.* Keep breathing. Return your attention to your own heart center when you feel complete with that.

— Now, expand your awareness to include all beings in your immediate environment; then include the neighbors on your street; then include all living beings in your city and in your country; then all on Earth. Offer them loving kindness: *May you be happy, may you be free from suffering, may you know peace.* Do this for a few minutes.

— Finish this meditation by bringing your attention back to yourself. Just as you wish all beings to be well and free from suffering, repeat: *May I also be happy, may I also be free from suffering, may I also know peace.* Give yourself some deeper breaths and bring your awareness to your body and the environment you're in. Keep your eyes closed for a few more minutes and enjoy your state of being. When you feel complete, open your eyes.

Affirming Your Perfection

As you go throughout your day, turn your attention to your internal dialogue spontaneously or when you catch your reflection in the mirror. Notice what you say to yourself. How do you treat yourself? If you find that you're not being self-compassionate, say affirmations to offset negative self-talk.

Practice saying the affirmations below (or any you like) aloud or silently to yourself as you look into your own eyes in a mirror:

- *I am free, beautiful, and wise.*
- *I am lovable just the way I am.*
- *I will never leave you.*
- *I love you.*
- *I am kind, loving, and present.*
- *Life loves me.*

If you feel discomfort as you say these to yourself, stay with the sensations and continue the practice until you're fully able to experience loving yourself while gazing into your eyes. Notice what gets in the way of loving yourself. You may find that some emotion arises and when you simply bear witness it, that emotion is then released in the process. If you notice a painful thought arising, remember to address it as you did in the *Don't Believe Everything You Think* exercise.

Schedule of Practices and Exercises

Week Four: Suggested Daily Practices	
AM	Long, Slow, Deep Breathing: 3 Minutes
	Sitting Meditation:12 Minutes
PM	Loving Your Body: 5 Minutes
	Sitting Meditation: 10 Minutes

Additional Awareness Exercises	
Anytime	Loving Kindness Meditation: 10–20 minutes
	Don't Believe Everything You Think
	Affirming Your Perfection

Insights for Success

This week's practices and exercises illuminate and transform negative habits of how you think about yourself and others into loving acceptance. Many of the practices can be done spontaneously when you want to open your heart to others and to yourself. When you stay committed to this program, you can't help but experience some degree of falling in love with yourself. When you treat yourself as well as you would treat someone you care about, you take care of your body, sing love songs to yourself, and say nice things to yourself.

The *Loving Kindness Meditation* will help you recognize yourself as a loving and lovable person, fully capable of genuine warmth, sweetness, and a peaceful response to life. Practicing this meditation while focusing on someone with whom you have a difficult relationship causes that relationship to transform. It's also a great practice to use when you want to address suffering that you hear about in the world. Instead of feeling helpless, this meditation gives you a sense that you're helping relieve the pain of others in some way.

Stay consistent in your meditation practice and bear witness to whatever comes up. Question those painful thoughts you have believed. Practice the *Loving Your Body* and *Affirming Your Perfection* exercises to enhance your loving, compassionate relationship with yourself. Keep in mind that self-compassion and kindness are keys to becoming soul-centered.

○ ○ ○

INTIMACY: CONNECT TO YOUR SOUL

"At the heart of each of us, whatever our imperfections, there exists a silent pulse of perfect rhythm, a complex of wave forms and resonances, which is absolutely individual and unique, and yet which connects us to everything in the universe."

— GEORGE LEONARD, AUTHOR, EDITOR, AND EDUCATOR

After four weeks of meditating you're most likely feeling more aware and less stressed. Have you noticed that you're approaching situations, people, and even your meditation practice with more gentleness and kindness? Do you have a more open mind? You are probably discovering that your truest source of happiness, compassion, and peace is within you . . . and you are becoming soul-centered.

This past week you focused your loving attention on yourself through the *Loving Your Body* and *Affirming Your Perfection* exercises. You also challenged those beliefs about yourself that caused stress. Check in now with a self-assessment: How could you be kinder to your body or love yourself more? Do you feel more compassion toward yourself or others? With the *Loving Kindness Meditation*, you began to treat everyone with equal kindness, even if at first it was only in your mind. With continued practice, you will experience more confidence, and feel more included and inclusive.

Your focus this week is to become more intimate with who you truly are by establishing a connection to the deepest part of you—your soul. I believe this is the most important work you can undertake in your lifetime. You will learn another inquiry practice and a variation on your sitting meditation practice, the *Mantra Meditation*, which is my favorite practice for establishing ongoing communion with the soul. You may even find that you adopt the *Mantra Meditation* in place of the silent *Breath Awareness* exercise as your primary meditation practice.

What Is the Soul?

The soul has been talked about for centuries in the fields of religion, philosophy, and psychology. Some claim that the soul is your very presence or essence. Some think it's divine, and still others don't believe in its existence at all.

Ralph Waldo Emerson, the 19th century American poet and philosopher, once said, "Within man is the soul of the whole; the wise silence; the universal beauty, to which every part and particle is equally related; the eternal *one*. . . . We see the world piece by piece, as the sun, the moon, the animal, the tree; but the whole, of which these are shining parts, is the soul."

Emerson's thoughts about the soul were radical for his time. While at Harvard, Emerson began the Transcendental Club and gathered with other great thinkers of his day, including Henry David Thoreau. One of the topics they discussed in their meetings was spirituality, the kind that transcends the physical world. Rather than solely studying the doctrines of established religions, they pursued a spirituality that could only be realized by direct experience of what Emerson called the "eternal one."

Years later, Albert Einstein sought to prove the existence of this "eternal one." He dedicated half his life to finding a single theory to describe all the workings of the universe. Even as he neared the end of his life, he kept a notepad close by to jot down equations that might lead to this theory of everything, the source code, so to speak. The quest for such a theory is still the holy grail of quantum physics; today, some physicists actually think they've figured it out.

While there's still no clear consensus among modern physicists, some talk of the superstring field theory that suggests an underlying, nonmaterial, intelligent field that unifies every quality, fundamental force, and law of nature. They say this field is the source of all material reality, a space from which all things arise. They also declare that this field is one of awareness—subtle yet powerful, silent yet dynamic—a seamless web that weaves together all of the material and nonmaterial.

If this theory is true, then each of us is the individualized expression of this intelligent field, and we are interconnected by that field of consciousness. (I love that the word *consciousness* has no plural!) Doesn't the description of this field sound similar to the "soul of the whole" spoken about by Emerson?

Einstein echoed these same ideas when he said, "A human being is part of the whole, called by us the *universe*, a part limited in time and space. He experiences himself, his thoughts and feelings, as something separated from the rest—a kind of optical delusion of his consciousness. This delusion is a kind of prison for us, restricting us to our personal desires and to affection for a few persons nearest to us. Our task must be to free ourselves from this prison by widening our circles of compassion to embrace all living creatures and the whole of nature in its beauty."

○ ○

What Emerson, Einstein, and physicists call "the whole" or "the one" has been described by many other names in various religions and philosophies. These are only some of the terms: *consciousness, pure awareness, essence, source, Spirit, self, nonlocal field of intelligence, the unified field, God, creator,* and *creative intelligence.* In this book, I usually use the word *soul* (and sometimes the terms *the real you, your inner self,* or *your true nature*) to refer to an individual's expression of that whole, which is your very being, the deepest part of you.

Coming up with an exact description of the soul is challenging. This is partly because it's so subtle and unidentifiable through your senses, and partly because there are a lot of beliefs surrounding it that keep it a mystery. It may help to look first at what the soul *isn't*.

Your soul is not your ego, your personality, your self-esteem, or your self-image. It is not your body, your thoughts, your ideas, or your actions. It is not dependent on your socioeconomic status, religion, profession, grades, popularity, authority, mood, weight, age, address, nationality, or marital status. Leave that all behind and see what remains in order to understand your soul.

Your soul is your pure awareness, the presence that calls your body home, the presence that looks through your eyes. Your soul is the real you, the reader of the words, the thinker of the thoughts. When you ask yourself, "Who am I?" your soul is the one who is asking.

Whether you realize it or not, your soul is intelligent and connected to all things. It is a powerful yet subtle force, similar to gravity or electricity or magnetism. You can't feel it or see it, but it is real. The great pioneer of soul music, Ray Charles, had the same idea when he described the soul this way: "It's like electricity—we don't really know what it is, but it's a force that can light a room."

While you can't see gravity or electricity or magnetic fields, you know that they are real forces because you can experience their effects: Flip a light switch, and a lamp lights the room. Lay your pen on a slanted surface, and it rolls off onto the floor. When you infuse the qualities of your soul into your daily life, the effects are as real as the lightbulb turning on or the pen hitting the ground.

Where you find the most power is at the more subtle levels of creation, a concept reflected in quantum physics. When physicists explore more subtle levels in creation, they find more space and less matter and density. At quantum levels, they discover non-material waves and spaciousness.

To illustrate the power of the subtle, consider a twig you might pick up as you're walking in the woods. Snap the twig in half, and you hear a sound that indicates a release of energy. Now, if you were a physicist working at the quantum level, you'd be able to split an atom within that twig in order to create nuclear energy more powerful than the snapping of any branch. The more subtle levels you access in creation, the more power you can harness, and the more space you will find. This includes tapping into the subtle levels of your own awareness. Just as in physics, when you tap into your soul, you discover a subtle yet spacious and powerful aspect of yourself. When you tap into this power, meaningful transformation can occur.

Stress and the Soul

Regardless of the external world and its movements and measures, your soul is content and peaceful. The soul is powerful and ever present, though when you're feeling anxious, nervous, unstable, ill, distracted, confused, critical, or judgmental, it may be difficult to feel a connection to it. For me, stress was once such a huge component in my life that I didn't fully realize the existence of this other aspect of myself—that is, until I learned to meditate. Even for those who know what it feels like to commune with their soul, when too much stress accumulates in their nervous system, that connection can fade.

This lesson was reinforced for me when a highly successful businesswoman hired me to teach her and her friends to meditate. She told me she couldn't connect with her soul, saying despairingly, "My spirit is broken." She explained that she was depressed due to a recent breakup—she couldn't sleep without pills, she had no appetite, and she had no lust for life. Her expression was so flat and her eyes were so dull, it almost convinced me she was right.

Fortunately, it is simply not possible for a soul to be truly "broken." No amount of stress can ever permanently break, damage, or alter your soul; and you can always regain your soul-centeredness and connection through meditation. As I talked to this woman, I recalled words from the ancient Hindu text, the Bhagavad Gita, that describe the ever-lasting presence of the human soul: "Fire cannot burn it, water cannot drench it, wind cannot dry it, weapons cannot cleave it. It is never born and it never dies. It has no beginning or end."

When an event is physically, mentally, or emotionally traumatic, the stress response kicks in as a survival mechanism. As we discussed in Week Two, the effects of stress interfere with your mind-body connection, choking off the lines of communication and resulting in health issues or imbalances. Such accumulation of stress can also mask your awareness of your soul and its expression, preventing you from accessing your soul's qualities.

My student's spirit may not have been broken, but her connection to it *had* become clouded by the effects of the stressful breakup. Fortunately, she was able to reconnect through her new-found practice of meditation, one of the best remedies I know for what so often feels like a broken spirit.

Soul Unbounded

Sages and mystics have been exalting the soul's many attributes for centuries. Some of them include: *creative, equanimous, wise, intelligent, generous, abundant, love, peace, purifying, authentic, efficient, magnetic, silent, dynamic, clear, powerful, confident, joyous, invincible, timeless, infinite, ever present, nourishing, balanced, spacious, still, immeasurable, evolutionary, expansive, flexible, stable, compassionate, harmonious, boundless, integrated, free, natural, organizing, radiant, simple, subtle, synchronous, whole, perfect,* and *interconnected.*

Yes, that is a long list, but if you'd like to get a glimpse into the power of these qualities, you can simply ask yourself this: *What would my life be like if I were _____?* Fill in the blank with any one of the attributes from above. Being soul-centered means connecting to and radiating these soul qualities in your life. Even if you weren't convinced that the soul is real, you could see how integrating such qualities into your life would be enriching.

Your body exists during a certain time period and takes up a certain location in space, but the same isn't true of your soul. Your soul is timeless and unbounded, existing beyond your sensory fields. Your body depends on its five senses—seeing, touching, tasting, smelling, and hearing—to figure out where things are in space and time, identifying and then separating objects in your environment. But this division doesn't exist in that field of consciousness that we talked about earlier, that one from which all things arise. That field is unbounded, beyond space and time, without divide. (Recall how Dr. Jill Bolte-Taylor discovered this when half of her brain went off-line.)

Maybe you've had the experience of spontaneously transcending time and finding yourself in the eternal now. Maybe you've had a glimpse into the realization that "you" and "I" are just words that separate us from the "we," our original state of interconnectedness. Maybe for a moment you've known the songbird, the breeze, the blue sky, and the cypress tree are not different from you. In or out of meditation, you can glimpse this interconnection of all things—when you do, you experience the intelligence and synchrony of creation.

○ ○

Many years ago, my now husband, Marty, was a young father of two and under constant pressure as the sales and product-development manager for a gift company in Boston. One day, he began to experience a tremendous amount of tension in his chest and went to the doctor to have it checked out. As far as the doctor could tell, Marty was totally fine. The doctor told him not to work so hard, and Marty left, feeling relieved. But a few days later, the pressure in his chest returned and was even more severe.

One of Marty's friends worked for Dr. Herbert Benson, a well-known cardiologist and a pioneer in mind-body medicine. He wrote the bestseller *The Relaxation Response* in 1975, which was one of the first books to integrate meditation into medicine and study it scientifically. Marty got an appointment with the famous doctor a few days later, and Dr. Benson put him on the treadmill for a stress test. Marty reported that he wasn't feeling well, and there was definitely something going on inside his chest. Dr. Benson looked at the results, then brought Marty into his office to explain that nothing was physically wrong with him—he just needed to relax.

At 31, Marty had been meditating daily since he was 18, so he was ready when Dr. Benson guided him through his famous relaxation technique. The doctor asked him to sit comfortably and relax, breathing in easily and naturally through his nose. He told Marty to hold the breath in for a second; then, as he exhaled through his nose, he was to silently say the word *one*. He and Marty breathed and meditated like this for several minutes. Marty felt wonderful as he returned to his office.

He'd been back at work only a few minutes when his phone rang. It was his younger brother calling to tell him that their mother was in the hospital suffering from a heart attack, and that Marty should come to New York right away. When Marty hung up the phone, the tension and pain he had been feeling in his chest instantly drained out of his body. He believed that he had been experiencing the distress his mother had been in for the last few weeks, though he'd been completely unaware of her difficulty until that point.

His mother's heart attack led to a three-month coma, and she awoke without the ability to talk or move any of her limbs (although her eyes were expressive, and she could make sounds and swallow on her own). Marty's father moved his wife home as soon as he could and hired round-the-clock nurses. Even though his wife couldn't speak, Marty's father believed she understood everything he was saying. For the next 13 years, he spoon-fed her two meals a day and had an ongoing conversation with her, laughing and joking no matter what her facial expressions were. She died peacefully after dinner one night, six years before I met and married her son.

I think this story of my husband's parents is remarkable, and a wonderful example of how, when you meditate, you can experience a true connection with anyone. That's because in meditation, you transcend your awareness of your environment, body, emotions, judgments, personality, ego, and self-image. You go beyond the world of form, phenomena, time, and space. You transcend it all, until you have the direct experience of the silent field that underlies all activity, and you connect with that which is your essence. When you practice meditation regularly, you have this experience again and again, even if it is only for an instant at a time in meditation. You also glimpse your soul's presence in your daily life, too—when you feel courageous, peaceful, inspired, clear, or compassionate. You establish a deep connection with that aspect of you not bound by the body, time, relationships, or circumstance: the "soul of the whole."

Soul-Centered vs. Ego-Centered

Becoming soul-centered is an inner journey that leads to a big shift. It's not that you reject the outer world and its meaning and importance; instead, you change the reference point by which you navigate life. A great way to make this change is through meditation, during which your center point naturally shifts from transitory experiences and reorients to your ever-present soul. You then carry that awareness wherever you go, in and out of meditation.

As meditation reconnects you with your own soul, it allows you to maintain perspective and gives you the ability to recover from life's strong winds. If you're thrown off balance by a thought or experience, you'll quickly realize it and regain your peace. You might then worry if your reference point shifts back and forth from soul-centered to ego-centered. But don't worry. Eventually your soul's presence will become dominant and more accessible, giving you a true integrity and strength from within. You will trust yourself and feel safe and confident wherever you go and whatever you do, because your reference point is your own soul.

When you're soul-centered, your self-worth is independent of others' opinion of you. You know that not only are you okay . . . but so is everyone else. It no longer matters who does or does not approve of you, what anyone thinks about you, or what they say you should or shouldn't do. When you're soul-centered, you access a deep inner wisdom and knowing that allows you to make decisions easily, confidently, and independently; you truly march to the beat of your own drummer.

Being dependent on external circumstances, including others' opinions of you, as the basis of your self-worth is to be co-dependent and the opposite of soul-centered—that is, ego-centered. You can test where your reference point is right now: When someone asks "How are you?" is your response dependent on your environment? Is your self-worth based on how you look, your bank account balance, your status, the state of your relationships, or what other people think of you? When you're ego-centered, you're mainly concerned with your self-image, with power and control, and with the approval of others. So you might feel fine when your life is doing well in these matters, but no external, ego-based cue is permanent; depending on them for security will give you a very unstable ride through life.

In contrast, when you're soul-centered, your reference point is your own soul rather than some outside force. There's freedom from fear, from the compulsion to control, and from needing validation from others. You experience the steadiness and harmony of your own spirit. The struggle for gaining approval and power begins to fade. You can tell when your reference point shifts back to co-dependence because wanting external validation creates anxiety, worry, and distraction. The awareness exercises you've been doing for the past four weeks will allow you to check in on your emotional state, an important tool to gauge where your reference point is.

One way to ascertain whether you're soul- or ego-centered is to see how quickly you judge others. When you hear that someone has found happiness or success, are you happy for that person or do you begrudge him or her? Does the news create a sense of instability in you, or are you generally joyful?

When you truly rejoice in the happiness of another, it creates peace of mind. There's no word for it in English, but it is referred to as *mudita*, or sympathetic joy, in yoga and Buddhist philosophy. Mudita is defined as an active delight that arises when you hear of others' good fortune, and it's considered a rare and beautiful quality. There's an endless supply of joy and happiness in the world, and it's available to each one of us. When you celebrate another's happiness, it enlivens peace, harmony, and kindness for all.

Sounds and Silence: Mantras

In silence, you find your soul's true home. But it may be hard to find that home when you have up to 50,000 thoughts a day . . . sometimes one every two seconds! Thoughts can overshadow your awareness of this silence, especially when you have the same thoughts over and over again for years. Thoughts start from the moment you wake up in the morning—*I slept well, I didn't sleep well, I have to hurry, What will I wear today?*—and go on and on, all day long, with or without your permission. It seems impossible to stop them, even though you may try to think about not thinking.

Practicing certain forms of meditation, especially sound meditation, can help you discover the silence that underlies those thoughts. This week, for your 30 minutes of meditation, you will focus on a sound, a word you repeat silently to yourself, known as a mantra.

The word *mantra* is Sanskrit and can translate to "instrument for the mind." Mantras can be used in a variety of ways: to evoke a feeling as in a devotional chant, to create a blessing, or as a vehicle to settle the mind. Mantras can be spoken, sung, silently contemplated, or listened to (when repeated by another). Sometimes mantras are even carved into rocks for ceremonial use. Mantras can be used with eyes open or closed. They can be used in sitting meditations, while in activity (such as when Tibetan Buddhists chant a mantra while they walk), or while in prayer (such as when people keep count with beads, like a rosary).

Mantras are found in nearly every culture and religion. They can be prayers, such as the Lord's Prayer in the Christian tradition, and the *om mane padme hum* mantra of Tibetan Buddhism. You may be familiar with the Christian mantra, *maranatha,* translated from the ancient Aramaic to mean "Come, O Lord"; or the Hebrew mantra, *hallelujah,* meaning "Praise God." Some people repeat the name of God as a mantra in the Judaic and Islamic traditions, or call the name of a saint as in the Catholic tradition (like in the "Ave Maria"). Mantras can also be words that people repeat to enliven a feeling in their life (such as "peace" or "all is well"), or a phrase (such as "Thy will be done").

The simple *Mantra Meditation* you'll learn this week is an ancient technique using a sound you repeat silently. It builds upon the other silent meditations you've been doing since Week Two, but instead of focusing on your breath, you'll focus on a mantra. When you practice meditation in this way, your awareness effortlessly and naturally transcends thoughts and body awareness, and you directly connect to your soul—that part of you beyond your ego, self-image, or personality.

○ ○

Let me explain how mantras work. As you go about your day, you are thinking in words. Right now, reading this, you hear your inner voice saying the words you're reading. Each word or thought has two components: (1) the meaning of the word and (2) the way it sounds, or how it looks when written (its symbol).

We can use the word *Hawaii* as an example. Say *Hawaii* to yourself a few times, slowly. *Ha-wai-i.* You'll notice that when you say the word repeatedly, it begins to lose its meaning and simply becomes a sound. But when you first read the word *Hawaii* on this page, it probably evoked some image in your mind. This is because the symbols you see on the page and the sound you hear when you say it are intrinsically connected to the definition of the word. *Hawaii.* When you first read it, you may have thought about a picturesque spot where you once vacationed, or come up with ideas of what it might be like (perhaps imagining umbrellas and piña coladas). Each person goes on his or her own trip with words. This is because the meaning of a word or phrase leads to an idea, or another word or phrase with their own meanings, then another, and so on. Those associations constitute much of your thought activity.

In meditation, repeating a mantra helps settle your nervous system, because when you focus on a word that has little or no meaning, the normal stream of thoughts is interrupted. When you focus on the actual sound of the mantra, and its subtle vibration, this also settles the mind. Instead of letting your thoughts take you on a ride, your thought process gets interrupted. The ride stops, or at least calms down, because your mind has no ideas to grasp onto. As a result, your thoughts become subtler and subtler, and eventually your awareness merges with the silence that lies under and between each thought. Dropping into this field of silence is sometimes referred to as going into "the gap." This gap is a conscious field, the same "one" from which all sounds and thoughts arise that the transcendentalists talked about.

Although understanding the concept of oneness can be challenging, you don't need to know all about it in order to meditate, to directly experience who you truly are, or to gain the benefits of your practice. The late Robert Adams, an American spiritual teacher who lived in Sedona, had this to say about the transcendence that happens naturally in meditation: "True silence means going deep within yourself to that place where nothing is happening, where you transcend time and space. You go into a brand-new dimension of nothingness. That's where all the power is. That's your real home. That's where you really belong, in deep Silence where there is no good or bad, no one trying to achieve anything. Just being, pure being. . . . Silence is the ultimate reality."

In meditation, your mind and body naturally calm down; your awareness transcends thoughts, emotions, and body sensations; and you experience a period of time where you aren't thinking anything. This experience of transcendence in meditation is so subtle and often so fleeting that you might not even notice that your internal conversation stopped for a moment. But it does.

This is when you are slipping into the gap. This is where (though it's not a place) you connect with *you,* your awareness, your soul. The frequency and duration of this transcendence depends on the state of your body and mind—how much stress you've been under that day, what you ate, how you slept, and so on.

In this state of transcendence, there's a peacefulness, expansion, and complete contentment. You're filled with a sense of total connection, safety, love, and joy; anything seems possible. Time passes without notice. A minute in the gap might seem like an hour, yet an hour might seem like a minute as well. You lose body awareness, too. But then, the moment you have a thought like *Where am I?* or *I could meditate forever—I feel great!* you are no longer in that gap, though you might have just been. That's because thoughts exist in time, and the gap is timeless, without thought.

Thoughts in meditation are an indication that you are releasing stress. Remember, as we talked about in Week Two, the content of the thoughts doesn't matter much, as they're usually about mundane things. Instead, it's the activity of having a thought that indicates you are releasing stress. And the more stress you release, the more you can connect with your soul. When you notice the thoughts, refocus on the practice at hand, and you will naturally transcend the thinking process and slip into the gap once again.

You can't reach the gap or transcendence by trying to get there or by thinking your way there. It happens naturally and only when you meditate without effort as you go from activity to silence. You can't hold on to the experience of pure awareness, because it isn't a "thing." You can't go "there," because it isn't a place to be. It is the experience of "the one" that is the source of everything.

If your approach to life has been "I'll believe it when I see it," I suggest you try shifting to "I'll believe it when I *experience* it." You won't be able to help but notice the effects that regular transcendence can bring to your life: you'll radiate your soul's qualities and experience a deep intimacy with your true nature.

A Meditator's Story: From Ego to Soul

Roland, a superior-court judge, attended a meditation workshop with me in Sedona in 2007. A few years earlier, his cardiologist had given him some bad news: his heart muscle had thickened to where it had become a serious threat. A stroke was imminent—not a matter of *if,* but *when.* Even so, it wasn't really Roland's personal choice to learn to meditate. He arrived at my class because he'd agreed to accompany a friend who was reluctant to come by himself, because "meditation isn't a guy thing."

Looking back, we joked that Roland was the "Accidental Meditator," but the stress he was under at the time wasn't funny. Known by the lawyers in his courtroom as "Judge Meany," Roland had a reputation for being short-tempered, unforgiving, and inflexible. He'd practiced law for 30 years as a public defender and then as a judge assigned to criminal court. He was overweight and on medication for his high blood pressure, a condition he attributed to his physical and emotional "inflexibility."

"I had an attitude that I knew better than anyone else what was best," he told me, looking back on his pre-meditation days. "I couldn't be flexible and step back to listen for other possibilities. I had to be right, so I couldn't hear what anyone else had to say."

Roland attended three of my meditation retreats that year. He admitted that he didn't keep a consistent practice at first, but he started to see benefits right away. He went on a weight-loss program and began working on his personal issues by attending advanced trainings and retreats to reduce stress. His blood pressure dropped, the weight came off, and he was no longer chastising lawyers in his courtroom for circumstances they couldn't prevent.

Then in 2008, Roland took on the most stressful case of his career, a high-profile murder case in which 8 people had been killed and 20 wounded. The trial spanned 11 months, during which time Roland received a new medical diagnosis: prostate cancer. "Had I not been meditating," he told me, "my reaction to the diagnosis would have been lots of ranting and raving, then total denial."

Instead, Roland signed up for radiation treatments and sought alternative therapies, demonstrating an openness he never would've had before becoming a meditator. He used a visualization exercise every time he went for radiation, seeing a blue healing light fill his body and zap the cancer cells. Today he is cancer-free and attributes his recovery to the realization that he could respond mindfully—not just react—to life's stressful events.

Reflecting on that difficult time, Roland said, "I've learned everything happens at exactly the right time—not when I think it should happen. I was ready, after two years of meditating, to hear that I had cancer. I had the frame of mind to deal with it. I knew that you can either accept how life is unfolding or resist it."

Today, Roland is cancer-free. He's also soul-centered. He told me, "I used to be defined by my role as a judge—I wanted to be the smartest judge, the hardest-working judge. But now I've learned how to surrender, to not have to be in control all the time, to go with the flow. Today, I'm just me, not so driven by how good of a judge I am. I no longer need to come out on top or grab the glory. I can choose what I do, and I choose to be just me."

A soul-centered judge! Wouldn't you like to meet one of *those* if you had to go to traffic or small-claims court? Today, Roland lives from his deepest essence—beyond his roles and public image— rather than following the demands of his ego. He has become a certified meditation teacher. He no longer works in criminal court; instead, he transferred to juvenile court where he can have an impact on young people before crime becomes their way of life.

In making the shift to being soul-centered, Roland began to embody the innocence and openness of a beginner's mind. When we last talked, he was excited about a State Bar of Arizona conference, where he would be leading a breakout group on how meditation improves the practice of the law. He said, "If you would've told me five years ago that I'd be doing what I'm doing today, I would've said you were crazy! My life is truly unrecognizable, and I know meditation opened the doors for me. In the past, I was myopic in my thinking; I believed I knew all there was to know. Now if I can *unlearn* something every day, I'm thrilled. I'm aiming at getting rid of all my judgments, preconceptions, and prejudices—all the stuff that has clouded my view."

When I see transformations such as Roland's, I have to ask myself, "Is there any doubt that meditation can change the world?"

Practices and Exercises to Cultivate Intimacy

Mantra Meditation

The *Mantra Meditation* is an ancient practice, one that many of my students stick with as their primary technique. The mantras you'll use in this meditation are from the ancient language of Sanskrit and are based on the subtle sounds of your breath. The sounds of inhalation and exhalation are linguistically represented, formed into the words: *ham* (pronounced like "hum") and *sah*. You'll use them silently in this meditation.

During this sitting meditation, you don't focus on the meaning of the sounds; rather, you rest your attention on the *sound* of the words as you think them: *ham* as you inhale, and *sah* as you exhale. You think these sounds without enunciating or saying them aloud. Instead it's almost as if you are *listening* to them repeat with each breath. When you do this practice without effort, it can interrupt the monologue in your head and naturally settle down your thinking process.

This week, use the mantras only in your meditation, not while in activity; and practice for 15 minutes at a time. (After this week, you can use the *Mantra Meditation* for however long you like, up to 30 minutes twice a day.)

Here's how you do it:

— Find a quiet, comfortable place to meditate. Set a timer for your predetermined time, and sit comfortably with your back straight but not rigid. Let your eyes close. The idea is to be still, but you may shift as needed to be comfortable.

— With your eyes closed, take a moment to notice the different sounds that become apparent to you, and welcome them.

— Scan your body with awareness, head to toe, relaxing as you go.

— Breathe naturally through your nose. Notice the movement of your breath in your body. Don't control or regulate the breath, simply be aware of its sensations for a few minutes.

— After a few minutes, on your inhale, gently, slowly think the word *ham*. Then as you naturally exhale, think the word *sah*. Keep your focus on the sensation of your breath while silently repeating the mantra.

— After a few breaths, gently draw your breath along the back of your throat, listening for the sound of *ham* in your actual breath. As you exhale, listen for the sound of *sah* as your breath is amplified in your throat.

— Let your breath return to its natural depth while you allow your mind to become absorbed in the sound or vibration of *ham sah* as you repeat it. There's nothing to figure out, no need to try hard, and nothing to control.

— Easily return your awareness to your mantra whenever you notice your attention has drifted away from it. It doesn't matter how many times you lose the focus—it could be very frequently. Don't try to stop the thoughts; instead, once you notice your attention has been carried away by them, gently reintroduce the mantra with your breath again, allowing the mantra to become predominant. Be kind to yourself. Don't push away or try to control your thoughts; simply refocus your attention. Remember, thoughts have nothing to do with how deep you are going or whether you are doing it "right."

— Continue meditating this way for 15 minutes (or the amount of time you've chosen to practice before you sat down).

If you notice that you are waiting for something to happen, treat this as any other kind of interruption, and refocus once again on the sound of the words you're silently repeating.

— To end your session, simply stop thinking the mantra. Take your attention off your breath, and sit with your eyes closed in the stillness for at least two minutes. After a minute you may gently stretch your body. Say a prayer, repeat affirmations, or continue to sit in the silence. You can even lie down for a while. Whatever you do, don't get up and make sudden movements. It is very important to take a couple minutes before jumping back into activity. After doing so, slowly open your eyes.

— *Optional:* Instead of repeating the *ham sah* mantra, you may prefer to silently count your breaths. Don't change the rhythm of your breath; count along in a relaxed fashion, as if you were listening to the numbers in your mind. Label an inhalation as 1, the exhalation as 2, and continue to silently count your breaths until you reach 10. Once you reach 10, begin again at 1 with the next inhalation. If at any point you realize you've lost count, then gently and nonjudgmentally restart from 1. It can be challenging to make it to 10, so be kind to yourself. Another option is to repeat the word *in* as you inhale and *out* as you exhale. Whichever method you choose, practice it for the entire 15 minutes.

Self-Inquiry: Who Am I?

There was a wise man from south India, Ramana Maharshi, whose followers would ask him all sorts of spiritual questions. He often responded to questioners with another question, such as, "From where did that thought arise?" or "Who is thinking the thought?" He also taught that the way to quiet the mind and to experience your own true nature is to ask the question, "Who am I?" The fact that you can question yourself and your thoughts means there is a thinker of the thoughts: the one who is experiencing the thoughts. By simply asking the question you connect with this aspect of you, your soul. This next practice has you ask that same question of yourself before you proceed with your sitting meditation.

Here's how to begin:

— Sit comfortably. Let your body settle and relax. Keep your eyes closed or capped (gazing softly toward the ground about three to four feet in front of you, focusing on nothing in particular).

— Practice *Long, Slow, Deep Breathing* for a few minutes.

— Now, let your breath be soft and natural.

— Ask yourself this question silently: "Who am I?" Don't answer the question with your mind; instead, ask, wait, and listen. Be comfortable with the silence and the unanswered question. You might hear an answer right away, you might not hear anything at all, or you might feel something. Let go of expectations and be present for a few minutes.

— Ask yourself again.

— Don't make up an answer. Instead, maintain a beginner's mind. The answer might meet your question now, later today, a week from now, or in á month. The answer might come in meditation or in activity. The most important part of this exercise is to ask the question, not answer it.

— After you sit in silence for a few minutes, let go of the question and any answers you might have heard in your mind. Continue with your meditation practice without further thought of the inquiry.

Walking with Awareness

When I lived at the Zen Mountain Center, we practiced *Walking with Awareness* between sitting meditation periods. It's a great opportunity to feel and experience your body in action while anchoring your awareness in the present moment. This walking meditation can release the stress that builds up when you sit for long periods of time.

Do this practice by itself, or before or after your *Sitting Meditation*. Find a quiet, private spot inside or outside. It doesn't have to be a large area. Determine the path you'll walk, either back and forth or in a circle. I like to do this while winding my way through the pathways of a labyrinth, when I find one. *Walking with Awareness* can help quiet the mind and body, anytime. This is different from *Walking Without Labels*. Here's what you'll do:

— First, determine how long you will be doing this practice before you start. You can do this for 5 or 15 minutes, or longer, if you like. Note the time or set a timer. You can practice with your eyes open or capped.

— Begin by standing where you are, and giving attention to your breath and your body. Feel the support of your breath, body, and the earth. Relax your face, shoulders, belly, and legs. Really relax.

— Start by taking a short step. Move gently, slowly. The movements will be very deliberate, taking a step every three seconds or so.

— Don't focus on a particular destination; just move, gently placing one foot in front of another.

— While in motion, feel each foot as it lifts and moves and makes contact with the ground. Pay attention to the alternating patterns of contact and release and balance. Notice your body weight shift and the movements of your feet, legs, and hips.

— Softly focus ahead and notice what meets your senses: what you see, hear, feel, and smell.

— Walking slowly might bring up emotions: you might get bored or feel frustrated because you want to walk faster or you dislike not having a destination.

— Consider repeating a phrase such as, "I have arrived" or "This is it" as you take each step. These phrases help counteract a destination-focused mind, helping you realize that each moment is itself the destination.

— Notice any sensations in your body. Don't cling to them or push them away; simply experience them, nonjudgmentally.

— When you notice your attention drifting away to some other place or time, remind yourself to focus on your body and its sensations. Stick with it. Be kind to yourself.

— When you are complete, come to a natural halt—not a sudden stop. Experience yourself standing still. Feel your body's weight as it sinks down your legs through the soles of your feet into the earth. With a slow, deep breath bring the session to a close.

Cultivating Sympathetic Joy

To cultivate *mudita,* sympathetic joy, notice how you feel when you learn about another's happiness or success. The other person can be anyone: a celebrity, politician, co-worker, friend, or family member. Do you compare your life to his or criticize yourself? Do you judge him or belittle his success?

If your reaction is less than kind toward them or yourself, simply notice how it feels in your body. By noticing and being aware of the discomfort, you can shift to a more generous response.

Greed, competition, and comparison are qualities of your ego. Abundance, generosity, and sympathetic joy are qualities of your soul. You can cultivate and enliven these traits by simply being aware of your mental habits, and then choosing a more soul-centered, loving response over an ego-centered perspective.

Schedule of Practices and Exercises

Week Five: Suggested Daily Practices	
AM	Self-Inquiry: Who Am I?: 3 Minutes
	Sitting Meditation: 12 Minutes
PM	Walking with Awareness: 5 Minutes
	Mantra Meditation: 10 Minutes

Additional Awareness Exercises	
Anytime	Cultivating Sympathetic Joy

Insights for Success

You might ask yourself "Did I do it right?" after completing the meditations and exercises on the last few pages. Rest assured that if you practiced the meditations easily and effortlessly, maintained a beginner's mind, were kind to yourself, and didn't give up, then you indeed did it right. The only thing you can do wrong is trying too hard to achieve a particular experience or come up with a certain answer when you ask a question—and even *that* isn't really wrong. In the *Self-Inquiry*, it's perfectly normal not to hear an answer to the question "Who am I?" right away. If you keep asking, you will hear a response. You'll activate a sense of your own presence simply by asking the question.

The goal in meditation is not to have mystical experiences, but simply to do the practices and exercises. Of course, you may have had thoughts, emotions, or physical sensations while you did them. By now you know that these are normal experiences in any meditation.

In the *Mantra Meditation,* you may have noticed a moment when you weren't repeating the mantra, you weren't aware of your breath, and you weren't thinking anything. You may have had the sense of being in a dreamlike state, somewhere between being asleep and awake or falling asleep. This is often the case when someone is in a restful awareness state—some call it "being in the gap." Although it can feel a little like sleep, it's not. Although in both cases you can get deep rest and are unaware of sensory stimulation, your awareness is dulled when sleeping. You might not hear someone call your name while you're sleeping, but you'd hear them while you meditate. This is because meditation leads to a restful *awareness* state, not a state of dullness or grogginess.

You may not notice that you were in the gap in meditation; even so, you probably were for a short time, especially if you have an expanded, blissful feeling. You cannot will your way to transcendence, because it's a natural outcome of the effortless meditation process, one that involves letting go rather than trying to make something happen. The practices themselves, no matter what your experiences during them may be, will move you toward a soul-centered life.

Meditation is like diving in a pool. You emerge covered not with water, but with the aspects of your soul. As you regularly take that dive from the waking state of awareness into the more settled meditative state, you integrate the soul's qualities. Eventually, this communion with your inner self allows your soul to radiate from within and the qualities to become infused into every aspect of your life.

○ ○ ○

AUTHENTICITY: COMMUNICATE HONESTLY

"Happiness is when what you think, what you say, and what you do are in harmony."

— MOHANDAS GANDHI,
LEADER OF INDIA'S INDEPENDENCE MOVEMENT

Last week's focus and meditation emphasized going beyond the material world and your identification with your environment, body, thoughts, self-image, memories, and desires in order to journey to your soul center. As you continue to enliven your soul connection, you become clearer about who you are and more attuned to your inner guidance. When faced with a choice, you tap into that guidance easily, learn to trust it, and feel more confident about expressing yourself.

The meditations and exercises you've learned thus far can be practiced on your own to create intimacy with your inner realm. But since most of us don't live a solitary life, the final three weeks of this program emphasize how to share yourself authentically in the world. The focus this week is on navigating your life using your internal guidance system, paying attention to your own wisdom, responding with integrity to opportunities that present themselves, and exploring the value of your attention while in communication with others.

Your Flexible Brain

Throughout this program, you've probably become more aware of your habits and routines. Some serve you, and others don't. Aging may play a factor as to why certain behaviors become established. As you mature, your brain becomes more rigid and develops well-worn pathways that can dictate your behavior. Do you habitually grab the phone when it rings, step on the gas when you see a yellow light, or make the same choices again and again? Routine reactions like these could actually be blamed on an aging brain.

Fortunately, science shows that meditation helps your neurons create new connections, and this makes it easier to let go of habitual behaviors. This realm of research concerned with the brain's flexibility is called *neuroplasticity*. A flexible brain helps you gain new perspectives and respond creatively to situations, people, and things.

As you meditate, you become more aware of the gap, that field of silence that underlies your normal thinking process. The same silence that exists between your thoughts also exists between each choice you make. As an example, imagine that you're eating at one of your favorite restaurants. The waiter comes over, and you place your order. If your mind is peaceful and calm, you notice there's a moment before you speak in which you could make a different choice, *any* choice; if not, you go with your habitual response. This moment of choice exists within every action of your life, even when you don't notice it.

As you become more sensitive and settled, you naturally have more access to respond creatively instead of habitually. You become aware of the moment when you have unlimited choices. For instance, when the phone rings, you don't *need* to pick it up right away, even if that's been your habit. You can choose, for example, to give yourself a deep breath or send loving energy to the caller, even if you don't know who it is.

This kind of creative response is available anytime, and it can help change your perspective. You could do something as simple as parking your car in a different place or enter a building through a different doorway than usual. If you feel yourself tensing up in the middle of an argument, you might choose a new response rather than defending your position. You could hear yourself say, "You might be right," to your spouse or co-worker, which relaxes your body and diminishes your defensive fighting habit. These are tiny changes, but each one illustrates that in any given moment you can choose to do just about anything.

Intuition: Your Internal Guidance System

By spending time in silence and your practice every day, your awareness expands and the noise and distractions (both in and out of meditation) lessen. The spaciousness between choices and action can become more obvious. In that space and underlying silence, you discover that your inner guidance system—what some people call "intuition"—is very real. Intuition isn't intellectual; it doesn't rationalize or analyze. Instead, it is wise and knowing. Following your intuition takes practice, although anyone can learn to do it. It can be a trusty navigator and doesn't steer you wrong. As you trust it again and again, it clearly guides you on your journey, and your life unfolds in a magical way that you couldn't have even imagined.

The word *intuition* comes from the Latin *intuitio,* meaning *looking at.* Though some people are visually intuitive, intuition isn't always about seeing with your mind's eye. Some people hear their intuition as a quiet inner voice. Others feel a physical sensation in their heart or on their skin in response to a situation, question, or choice. My friend Victoria finds a bitter taste in her mouth when some choice or idea disagrees with her. I'm sure there are those who navigate their choices through the subtle sense of smell. Whichever way your own intuition makes itself known, it is communicating the path to follow toward real happiness, away from pain or danger.

Whether you use your intuition or not, you have it—everyone does, and at all times, too. You might not be aware of it because your intuition can be masked by stress in your body. Sometimes it is hidden under unexamined mental habits such as not trusting yourself, thinking you can't do something, or refusing to consider other ways because one way is how you *always* do it. Those tens of thousands of thoughts you have daily can distract you and shroud your intuitive voice. Commands like "Buy this!" or "Do it this way, and you'll be happier!" brought to us by the media don't help us get any clearer.

What if you truly listened to and followed your own inner guidance? What kind of life would you have? Many successful people know the value of relying on their intuition: Bill Gates, Oprah Winfrey, and Donald Trump are just three high profilers who attest to the value of it in creating their empires. Building up your intuition—one of the many benefits of meditation—would help you, too, achieve success . . . however you define "success."

Meditation quiets the mind so you can focus your attention where and when you want to; and that includes focusing on your intuition. When you use internal cues to guide you in your moment-by-moment choices, you see that intuition is an open communication—it's not controlling or emotional. Control, emotionalism, rationale, and logic are aspects of the mind and ego; whereas intuition is a wise, clear, steady communication from your soul.

Are you one of those people who ignores your intuition? Maybe you think that you know better. You overrun your intuition with your "rational" mind and notions of wanting to be right, in control, and powerful. A study conducted at the University of Toronto at Scarborough reports that people who can't talk themselves through a task aren't able to exercise the same amount of self-control that's possible when they do have an internal dialogue.

This study shows that accessing your inner voice actually helps your self-discipline and prevents you from making impulsive or habitual decisions. Not listening to your intuition means missing good direction.

○ ○

Following my own internal guidance system literally saved my life. Shortly after returning to California from my travels in India, I borrowed a friend's old Plymouth Valiant with balding tires. I was driving southbound on the freeway from the Zen Mountain Center outside of Idyllwild to La Jolla, a distance of about 100 miles. As I drove, I became aware of my inner voice; it was subtle but persistent, directing me to pull over as I moved along in the fast lane in rush-hour traffic. The calm, steady voice kept saying, "Pull over to the right. Get in the slow lane." I tried to ignore it, but after hearing it a few times, I put on my blinker and crossed lanes.

I had been driving in the right lane for only a few moments when my car suddenly spun out counterclockwise. It turned 360 degrees as it skidded across traffic to end up stopped by the center dividing median, still facing the right direction. I sat there for a moment, stunned. And as I waited for a break to reenter traffic, I realized that if I'd ignored my inner voice, the spinout would have taken my car across the median, through the guardrails . . . and into oncoming traffic. I have no idea what caused my car to do that, since I hadn't applied the brakes and the roads were dry. But I'm eternally grateful for listening to my inner wisdom that told me to pull over and slow down. Now, after that experience, I always heed that calm, steady voice in my head.

It does take practice to distinguish your intuition from your imagination or from the frenetic, critical voice that sometimes intrudes. But once you've developed the habit of listening and following its wisdom, you learn to recognize its language and come to trust in it. It's like finally trusting your GPS to take you where you want to go, and often the destination is so much better than anything you might have chosen logically or rationally.

Paying Attention to Your Yeses and Your Nos

What choices have you made that provide you with a temporary sense of satisfaction, or that "just make it easier for now"? It might seem simpler or better in the moment to say yes even though you hear a no (or vice versa), but it isn't in the long run. Your yes starts a chain of events that is harder to undo as it continues to unfurl, as was the case for two friends of mine, whom I asked: "Was there ever a time when your intuition clearly said no, but you went ahead anyway?" Coincidentally, each said that they'd heard an inner no while walking down the aisle to be married! Both ignored it and said yes because it would have been inconvenient to say otherwise: the big day had already arrived, the caterer had set up, and the guests were sitting in their seats. So they ignored their intuition, chalked it up to being nervous, and got married anyway. Both have since divorced.

Expressing yourself authentically depends on accessing your deep inner wisdom, your *truth,* and letting it guide you in your communications. This idea is exemplified in a very simple way in the book *Still Life with Woodpecker* by novelist Tom Robbins. As one of his characters explains it, "There are only two mantras . . . yum and yuk." It's binary really: something is "yummy" if you like it and want more (yes), and "yucky" if you don't like it and are repulsed by it (no). And based on this yum and yuck, you can either move away from or toward people, places, and things that arise.

When asked a question or facing a choice, ask yourself, "How does my body feel right now?" You can often count on your body to show you signs of comfort and discomfort. It doesn't lie: When you feel a tightening of your stomach or chest area, a sick sensation, or an impulse to cross your arms or move away, these are indicators of a yuck/no. When you feel lightheartedness, expansion, joy, or ease, that's a yum/yes. And as my hairdresser Isaac says, "If it's not a yes, then it's almost always a no."

A simple question I've taught my students to ask themselves when faced with a choice is, "Is it a yum or a yuck for me?" They immediately know. You will, too. Then you can respond with integrity, saying no to things, people, or events that are stressful; and saying yes only when you really mean it. There's no need to manipulate yourself to please people at the expense of yourself. When you stay in your integrity, it is good for both your relationships and your life.

A student of mine discovered this for herself, as she told me, "At Christmastime my husband, son, and I were invited to the East Coast for the holidays to be with my family and friends. I heard a distinct no/yuck about going on the trip, but I forged ahead because I didn't want to disappoint everyone. As soon as I got there, I became ill and spent the majority of my time cooped up in a bedroom.

"The trip had been a clear yuck for me, but I didn't listen. Trusting and actually following my intuition, despite what the world says or wants, is a real challenge. I'm learning that the more I move toward yum, the better my life becomes."

You might already be aware of how your body communicates with you and are able to distinguish your internal yes and no— but as my student learned, the key is to *act* on that communication, making choices based on your knowing. It sounds simple, but it can seem easier when you're in the moment to go against a strong inner feeling and talk yourself out of your intuitive answer in order to please someone else or meet others' expectations. But beware: each time you make the choice not to follow your inner wisdom, you dishonor yourself and your own integrity, and this causes stress.

Sometimes, however, you are presented with a seemingly impossible situation, when each option seems like a no and choosing either would cause pain. This is the time to remember the interconnection of all things, the intelligent source from which everything arises. When you're faced with a choice like that, know that there will always be a decision that's right for you. Feel the cues of your physical sensations; your body and heart are amazingly sensitive and will guide you to a decision that's right for all, no matter how painful that choice might seem. Practice aligning every choice you make with your inner knowing. I promise you, this will create an authentic and fulfilling life.

A Meditator's Story: Intuitive Choices

Allison came to a retreat to learn to meditate in the fall of 2010. At the age of 28, she struck me as a smart, attractive woman who was at a crossroads in her life. She'd obtained a dual master's degree in childhood education and counseling, and had a career managing educational-development programs for state government grants. Even with her success, she was at a point where she desperately desired change in her life. At the retreat, I asked the participants to choose a word as an intention during the weekend; Allison's word was *pivot* because she felt she needed to pivot the direction of her life.

She explained, "In my relationship, I was at a point where my husband and I weren't happy. We both knew things needed to change, but we were unable to take any action. It was a similar situation with my career: I got different job offers, but I'd just sit and think about them, having no idea how to respond. I would get so stressed out trying to decide, but no answers would come to me."

Life was overly busy for Allison before she started meditating, to the point that she felt her days were slipping by. "I'd get home at the end of a day and say, 'Wait a minute, what happened on my ride home?' All of a sudden I'd be in my driveway and couldn't even recall the ride. Time was going by, and I was not present. That's when I was motivated to become more mindful, and I decided to learn how to meditate."

Allison was already familiar with meditation, because her mother had practiced yoga while Allison was growing up. She herself started doing yoga at age ten, and had always been interested in Eastern traditions, like Buddhism. Still, she struggled to find her intuitive voice. As she described it, "Whenever I had a dilemma, I'd freeze. I had no idea what to do. I could never seem to identify what my authentic self wanted to say."

When I caught up with Allison a year after she'd attended my retreat, she told me how her new practice had changed her life. "It's so much better now, since I've been meditating regularly. I've come to accept that if there's no immediate answer, I don't have to get freaked out. I can accept more uncertainty, more ambiguity in my life. I feel more at peace with making decisions, because I can hear and trust my inner voice now."

Both her career and her marriage had shifted, and she made decisions more easily toward her goals. She and her husband amicably decided to take a "growth break": to go their separate ways for an agreed upon period of time. As for her career, that too was headed in a new and exciting direction. She said, "For me, the essence of meditation is about discovering how I can best be of help to the world and increase my own happiness at the same time. I thought about it, then moved into the field of international development; I now work with relief programs around the world. I've started my own business and even my own blog. I know what I want, and I'm doing what I need to do to make it all happen."

Today, as an aspiring global consultant, trainer, and workshop leader, Allison mentors others in the fields of early childhood education and mental health—especially cross-culturally. She anticipates traveling to Cuba, Haiti, Peru, Nicaragua, and Guatemala to work on her development goals for children—while still advancing her own personal growth.

She says, "Meditation has given me a consistent framework for starting my day. There's something comforting about the regularity of it, and it's becoming as routine as brushing my teeth. Regardless of where I am or what's going on in my career, I can bring the skills I've learned with me anywhere.

"In all of the life changes I've been making—including growing my business and negotiating my marriage—it's been stressful and scary at times. But the practice of meditation helped me be calm and overcome the difficulties. I've definitely learned to trust my intuition more. Meditation is affordable—and priceless!"

From an Ashram to the Zen Center

My personal journey spanned many states, countries, and continents; yet my inability to express how I felt and who I was followed me everywhere I went. I often didn't feel confident and was dependent on other people's approval in a very deep way. I never expected that days of silent meditation practice would be the necessary ingredient for building my self-worth and developing the ability to speak my truth.

I remember when I arrived in New York City in the middle of winter wearing flip-flops. I'd been traveling in India for six months, and pairs of my shoes had disappeared when I took them off to enter temples. I went looking for winter shoes along 6th Avenue, and was amazed to see so many choices in store after store. I felt out of place in my own country. During the time I was in India, imported goods were not allowed, so I was used to seeing only a few items to choose from no matter what I was shopping for.

The vast material abundance I encountered triggered a compulsion to find a job immediately, so I could earn money to buy all these things. It was an uncomfortable feeling, and I was surprised that I could so easily and quickly be hypnotized by the material world. Although my personality wanted these things, I could discern that my soul did not. I wasn't ready to join the traditional working world; I truly wanted to live a simple life and to continue what had become a deep and exciting adventure—exploring my spirituality. I wanted to live with like-minded people who knew that you couldn't purchase the best things in life: serenity, joy, love, healing, contentment, friendship, spirituality, awareness, peace, and nourishment.

A few weeks later, I moved into an 8' x 10' one-room cabin nestled below towering pines on a remote hillside at Yokoji Zen Mountain Center, a small meditation practice community off the grid in Southern California. The Center had been started by Japanese priest Taizan Maezumi Roshi at a time when his contemporaries, among them Shunryu Suzuki Roshi, were opening Zen training centers in California and New York.

I became a resident there to explore meditation in the Zen Buddhist tradition. Buddhism is more of a philosophy than a religion, contrasting greatly with the Hindu-based ashram and the Tibetan Buddhist nunnery that I'd been involved with in India.

I had visited the Zen Center on my days off for years, and being there now felt like home.

At the center, the daily routine was similar to those at a traditional Japanese monastery. It consisted of sitting meditations (*zazen*), walking meditations (*kinhin*), work practice (*samu*), and a communication practice. I was used to the long periods of silence and meditation, but "council practice" was new to me. Council was based on communication practices adopted from the Native American tradition called "The Way of the Council." The teachers (*roshis*) met with us residents regularly for community council on Sunday afternoons. As one of my teachers, Roshi Seisen Saunders, said, "The Way of the Council is a group meditation practice, a group *zazen*."

Freedom of Expression "In Circle"

Council, like sitting meditation, is where you deeply experience the present moment and anchor yourself in it, so you can experience what is happening in the now—whether it is silence, sounds, physical sensations, changes in the breath, emotions, or thoughts. Council is based on communications practices where you bear witness to thoughts and feelings as they arise and dissipate. Further, you not only bear witness to your own feelings, you also bear witness to one another's. You maintain a beginner's mind, allowing yourself to be present to whatever arises without labeling it or expecting it to be a certain way.

There are many reasons to gather in council, including mediating a conflict, coming to a decision, or addressing some unresolved issue. I have found that sitting in council can help heal addiction, co-dependence, shame, or any behavior that arises from having misconceptions about ourselves. At the Zen Center, the council practice was used mainly to address community and personal issues.

The council guidelines were simple. First we'd gather and sit in a circle. The teacher would hold a talking stick (or a feather, shell, or other ceremonial item) to initiate the discussion. When she finished speaking, it was handed to whoever was moved to speak. If no one was, the stick was placed in the middle of the circle until whoever was inspired to would take it. Before sharing, you would say your name to own what you were going to express. Whoever held the stick could speak without interruption. Those who weren't speaking would be silent yet emotionally present, listening wholeheartedly and taking responsibility for how they were feeling as they listened. This was all done with a sense of equanimity, not judging your own or someone else's expression, but simply bearing witness to it.

Other guidelines included speaking specifically rather than generally or abstractly, being respectful of someone else's process, and being able to rest comfortably in silence—our own or another's. We were also not to fix or "save" anyone in the circle, nor were we to give advice or set someone straight—I would notice prejudices that stirred within me and bore witness to any desire to control what was going on. If an issue arose with one of us as we sat in council, we didn't address it with the person outside of the circle. It was there to stay; that was our code of confidentiality.

The experience of being in council is explained in Jack Zimmerman and Virginia Coyle's book, *The Way of Council:*

> Compassion arises naturally when we listen with respect and express ourselves honestly with an open heart, whether it be in words, song, movement, or silence. Wisdom flows from the wholeness of the circle and reveals itself as the *truth of the council*. The expression of this truth can come through anyone in the circle or through the silence. Listening to the voice of the council teaches us that the circle's knowledge is greater than the totality of its members' individual knowing.

Often, being really listened to is enough to help someone find clarity or heal some deep wounds (as it did in my case). I was still ashamed of various parts of my personality, didn't completely accept myself, and was co-dependent on others for my sense of self-worth. But I found that by feeling a connection to those in the circle, it reduced the sense of separateness and isolation I'd had most of my life. I was breaking patterns that had formed in my early years when I hadn't expressed myself.

Being in council was my first experience of being heard by a group, other than when I was teaching a meditation or mind-body health class. They heard me and my opinions, ideas, and feelings; they trusted me simply because I was with them in the circle, and I trusted them, too. Whenever I was sitting in a circle, I felt safe, whole, and healthy. I loved being in the company of others who, like me, wanted to express themselves courageously and bear witness to each other. I learned to trust myself to feel what I was feeling in real time and express that honestly.

○ ○

After almost two years at the Zen Center, I moved to Northern California to work with Gary Zukav, author of the best-selling book *The Seat of the Soul*. We also gathered "in circle" there, supporting one another by listening as the most difficult of emotions were expressed.

Sometimes there would be long periods of silence. We'd wait until someone was "moved to speak," a term shared with the Quaker tradition. (In Quaker meetings, everyone sits quietly until someone feels a rush of energy, or "quake." This would be a sign that Spirit was moving through them, and they were about to express something important.) I trusted this process and the wisdom of the circle. I found that a wise insight would emerge if we sat there long enough, more potent than any one of us could've discovered alone.

The silence helped me focus on and become more aware of my own emotions, and also to bear witness to the expression of others'. We learned to express ourselves using "I" statements, which is a subtle, yet empowering shift to make. Many people take a more casual, other-focused approach, expressing themselves by using "you" instead of "I" when describing their personal experience.

However, using "I" is a more intimate self-expression and a key to reaching even deeper emotional levels.

When I communicated using "I" statements outside of the circle, I could say what I felt without blaming others or creating conflict. It was especially helpful for communicating with my boyfriend at the time. He couldn't argue with me if I simply shared how I felt and took full responsibility for it. Who can argue with "I'm feeling sad"? On the other hand, if I had said, "You're making me sad by doing this . . ." That's a completely different communication.

I also learned to speak from my heart and soul, rather than my intellect. The seat of my awareness began to shift from my head into my heart center. Sometimes this was a natural shift, and sometimes I consciously reoriented my awareness to the center of my chest (because that's where most of us point to when we refer to ourselves or say "I"). Anchored in this way, I felt more connected to myself and each person in the room. My transformation deepened, and I decided to be "in circle" no matter who I was relating to. Today, I continue to use what I learned in council in my interpersonal communications, and I share council practice in the meditation retreats I facilitate.

The Value of Your Attention

Your kind attention, given purely and openly, is the most concrete expression of love. What you put your attention on thrives, whether the object of your attention is yourself, your emotions, your body, your spirit, your relationships, your ideas, your desires, your family, your pets, your plants, or your environment. What you don't pay attention to withers and dies.

William James, the pioneering 19th century psychologist, expressed the value of attention when he wrote the following in *The Principles of Psychology* over 100 years ago:

> If no one turned round when we entered, answered when we spoke, or minded what we did, but if every

person we met "cut us dead," and acted as if we were non-existent things, a kind of rage and impotent despair would ere long well up in us, from which the cruelest bodily tortures would be a relief; for these would make us feel that, however bad might be our plight, we had not sunk to such a depth as to be unworthy of attention at all.

We've all experienced being "cut dead," meaning shunned, even if only for a few minutes. Anyone who has ever been hung up on in the middle of a phone conversation, ignored, left out, bullied, or given the silent treatment by someone or a group of people, has experienced it—this being denied a sense of belonging or even their own existence. Many indigenous tribes use social ostracism as the severest of punishments, which often leads to the death of the offender. Some of us even wage that upon ourselves when we practice self-ostracism, ignoring our own inner voice and hiding the expression of our own truth.

Withholding your attention from something can be as cruel an act as giving your attention can be loving. The attention I'm referring to is in no way negative, like that of criticizing, stalking, or abusing another. Nor is it the kind I was taught in the Army or in school when told to "Pay attention!" Instead, the attention I am talking about here is a gentle "attending to," like the kind of attention you give when you're hugging someone you love, reading your favorite poem, or watching a spectacular sunset. When you attend to others, yourself, and things around you, in that attending, in that *caring for*, there is love. Imagine it this way: love is attention and attention is love. Practicing this can transform the experience of your life.

As you develop the ability to engage your awareness on purpose, you experience a continuity, a flow, in the midst of the ever-changing scenery. Awareness of your own ups and downs, your reactions, your choices, and the shifting circumstances can become a constant. Giving loving attention to yourself, others, the moment, and the circumstances of your life can also become a constant. The possibility of experiencing love and awareness is available in every moment.

Listening to Others with Presence

Listening to your inner wisdom is an important component of being soul-centered, but equally so is listening fully and openly to someone else. Your presence is a gift you give to others. Being an attentive, soul-centered listener helps you have more harmony in your relationships. Being a good listener is more than just being silent when people are speaking; your presence creates a space where they can feel heard, where they can be authentic and express who they are.

There are times when others might have to say or ask for something that is difficult for them to express. When you are present and attentive to them through this, and are comfortable in silence as they find their voice, giving them the space and time to express themselves, they feel empowered and heard. Through the listening, people become more vibrant, clear, and beautiful; and their souls shine through.

After taking part in circles and having the experience of deep listening, I became keenly aware that most of us don't listen well to others. Although people may seem like they're listening, many are actually doing other things at the same time. Multitasking makes it difficult to truly be present for someone, and it doesn't go unnoticed. Consider these scenarios: Have you ever tried to communicate with someone who is texting or gazing in the mirror? Have you ever spoken with someone who appeared to be listening, but you had a sense that his or her mind was elsewhere? Have you had a conversation with someone on the phone who seemed as if he or she was disengaged and doing something else?

On the other hand, think of how *you* listen. While others speak, do you plan or rehearse what you are going to say next, or filter out what you don't want to hear? Do you get ready to give advice while they are speaking? Do you pretend to listen, but instead think of something totally different and miss the moment? Do you ask never-ending questions to shift the focus off of them and back onto you? Have you tried to rescue others from having to express what want by preemptively offering it, so they don't have to ask? Do you *interpret* what they say rather than listen to their actual words?

There are many reasons that we might listen in such a way. Perhaps you start daydreaming because of something they said and regain your focus halfway through their thought. Perhaps you feel competitive—or even proud that you "know" the solution to their problems—and can hardly wait to have them finish talking so you can share your brilliant idea. Maybe you've felt insecure around people so you interrupt them with a statement you think might impress them, or ask a million questions. These are the many subtle ways through which we don't listen. Paying attention to our attending is a wonderful way to be loving, and the practice of meditation can help you to be more aware of where and how you focus your attention

Someone once said, "Without the listening, there would be no music, no poetry, and no prayer." Listening nurtures the soul. Sometimes the deepest insights of the creative mind emerge once someone can simply be present to you and listen to you deeply. Think about someone who knows and loves you. How do you feel when he or she listens to you? We all desire the connection that communication creates. With practice, you can do that for anyone. The *Listening with Love* exercise that you will practice this week will help build up your skills to become a good listener.

Learning to Ask for What I Want

Earlier in this book, I told you how I left the huge snow drifts of Mount Shasta for the ocean vistas of Southern California to join Byron Katie's tiny staff. Once in the Los Angeles area, I found a house-sitting job and reaffirmed my commitment to love myself first before ever falling in love again. My inner romance bloomed. I even bought myself a beautiful ring to remind me of my commitment to myself.

I took myself out on dates: for coffee, to the movies, and even to dinner. I also had a standing date with myself each morning, before driving to work. I'd walk along the boardwalk or stroll barefoot on the beach. Sometimes, on purpose, I would drop my awareness to my heart center and meet people in this way as they passed me by. It was a very sweet experience.

The house I was living in also happened to be just one block up from Katie's ocean-view residence. I didn't know it then, but my future husband, Marty, watched me from her living room as I passed by on my morning walks to the beach. Marty was a friend of Katie's, visiting from Sedona, Arizona. He was a successful businessman who had helped her reorganize her company to operate more efficiently. It was a few months after his restructuring that I started working for Katie.

I met Marty for the first time when I brought some paperwork to Katie at her house. He and his daughter were sitting on the sofa, looking at brochures of nearby colleges. I saw that he was attractive and confident, and instantly thought to myself, *I'm not getting involved with anyone. Not now.* After all, I was learning to love myself, and I had my commitment ring on to prove it.

While waiting for Katie to finish up her work to meet with me, I sat down to talk to Marty and his daughter, Danielle. Conversation was easy. We discovered that we had lived a few miles apart in New York, where we had both been born. We then both moved to the Boston area, and there we'd lived within a few miles of each other for years. And we had a lot in common, including our dedication to our spiritual paths most of our adult lives.

I got to know Marty better as time went on, as he made frequent trips from his home in Arizona to California. He would call to see how work was going and how I was doing. I'd check in with myself: *How _am_ I doing?* I was doing well. I loved my job. I found more confidence; I loved and took care of myself. I also noticed how comfortable I felt talking to this man and being around him. Marty was light hearted and made me laugh and laugh. I felt fearless, saying things to him I never would have said if I worried about how others view me. I felt empowered, and the freedom of expression was exciting.

Marty had been a meditator for years and communicated honestly, too. It wasn't long before he revealed that he had seen me walking each day from where he sat in Katie's house, unaware then that I too was working with Katie. I'd caught his eye, he said, because I looked so confident and happy. I loved the serendipity: I was taking myself on dates to learn to love myself and become self-sufficient, and those exact qualities of self-love and independence were what attracted this man.

A few months later, we began a long-distance romance, traveling back and forth from Los Angeles to Sedona. I loved being loved and wondered: *Have I finally loved myself enough that I can enjoy another person loving me?* It seemed so, and the romance progressed without the usual co-dependency and loss of self I'd experienced so many times before. I felt totally free to be myself around him. Loving myself made all the difference. Marty told me that he found my truthful expression to be erotic, and appreciated my fearlessness, as he felt it was the key ingredient to being honest with each other in our relationship.

I was thrilled when Marty first said, "I can see us living together, being married." I was excited and felt deeply honored, a response I didn't feel in my past relationships. Then suddenly, his repeated remarks about our future together stopped appealing to me. Something didn't feel right, but I couldn't figure out what it was. One day, I was driving my old trusty Volvo to an appointment and talking with Marty on my cell phone. As he mentioned being married, I felt a surge of energy go through my body; it was so strong that I had to pull over. I was "moved to speak," but not sure what would come out. Even so, I trusted it.

"Marty, I hear you saying you can see us being married, but . . . " I hesitated, trembling slightly, because I was afraid to find out what would come out next. "You're going to have to *ask* me to marry you." He was silent.

Tears streamed down my face. They were tears of relief from speaking my truth, mixed with grief from the many relationships in which I'd never done that—all those years of ignoring my emotions to avoid facing rejection. My habit of not expressing myself created a lot of pain, but asking for what I wanted could also lead to pain—to a *no*. After an endless moment, Marty said sweetly, "I hear you."

I now understand that my tears were also the recognition that I was on my own side. It wasn't that I didn't want to get married; I simply wanted to be asked. I didn't want another relationship to develop unconsciously without choice and awareness, simply assuming it would go this way or that. And I wasn't going to let my fate be completely in the hands of another, no matter how much I liked the person or wanted him to like me. I needed to speak my truth and be an active participant in the way the dance played out—and that took courage.

Months later, after returning from travels in Europe with Katie and directing her School for The Work, Marty asked me if I would marry him. When he proposed, I didn't respond right away. Instead, I asked myself: *Would I marry him?* I thought I might say yes, but I waited until I actually felt the answer in my body. (Marty tells me it took at least a minute and a half.) I closed my eyes, and it was a *yes*.

We got engaged, which was a first for me. Although I had been married before, I'd never been engaged. Now I was in the engagement I'd longed for, a way of being "in circle" with each other. Ten years later, even though Marty and I are married, we are still "engaged" and share a relationship based on expressing ourselves honestly, deeply listening to each other, and asking for what we want. Listening to yourself and asking for what you want are practices that lead to a life of fulfillment, far beyond what you could ever imagine.

○ ○

Meditation helps you train your attention, so you can focus it where and when you want. Remember this law of quantum physics: by simply putting your attention on something, it shifts; it doesn't remain the same, it transforms. This theory can be applied to ourselves. Here's a simple example: when someone asks you how you are, rather than responding to them with "fine," give yourself a moment to check in with yourself. Really ask yourself how you are. Give yourself this attention. Habits like not saying what you mean, ignoring your feelings, or not asking for what you want can change with attention. When I focused on becoming more self-aware—feeling my emotions and expressing how I truly felt—that focus caused it all to shift.

This week, I invite you to see what you are attending to. I invite you to be a better listener. That means not only to be a better listener of others, but to truly attend to yourself. Observe and feel your emotions, listen to yourself, speak your truth, and ask for what you want. And when others ask you a question, take the time to feel into it and respond honestly. By resolving to clearly observe and put your loving attention on your habitual ways, they will shift naturally.

Practices and Exercises to Cultivate Authenticity

Heart-Centered Breath

Our hearts do much more than pump blood through our veins . . . they inform us with their intelligence and wisdom. There are as many neurons in the heart as in some sections of the brain; in fact, the heart's magnetic field is actually stronger than the brain's—5,000 times more! The heart sends signals to the brain that change the entire nervous system, reducing stress hormones, enhancing the immune system, and increasing antiaging hormones.

When you pay attention to your heart, you enliven its intelligence and its qualities of peace, love, compassion, joy, gratitude, and inclusiveness. The *Heart-Centered Breath* exercise is a way to bring your awareness into your heart center, and can be used anytime: while meditating, walking, or listening to someone else. It can be practiced by itself or as an adjunct to your regular *Sitting* or *Mantra Meditation*.

This week, practice this breath exercise before your *Sitting Meditation*. Here's how:

— Get into a comfortable seated position. Settle down. Your eyes can be open, capped, or closed. Scan and relax your body.

— Bring your attention to your breath as you breathe through your nose. Feel the sensations of the inhale and exhale of your breath, the coolness of your breath on the inhale, the warmth on the exhale. Don't try to control or regulate your breath or its rhythm. Let your body naturally settle.

— After a moment or two, bring your attention to the rise and fall of your chest. Imagine looking inward toward your heart. Let your attention rest there for a breath or two.

— Next, imagine your breath moving into and out of your heart center as if it were a doorway to your breath. (You can also place your hand over the center of your chest to keep your attention focused there.)

— Match the length of the inhale to the length of the exhale. Breathe in this rhythmic way for three or four full breaths.

— Now return your attention to the natural breath pattern without controlling the rhythm, depth, or speed. Continue imagining the breath moving in front of you—in and out of the center of your chest.

— Continue like this for a period of time, refocusing the attention on your breath when you notice it has shifted to something else. Be kind to yourself.

— When you are finished, sit in the stillness for a few moments before opening your eyes (if they were closed).

Listening with Love

This listening practice is to help you cultivate mindfulness while engaged in a conversation. The next time you're listening to another, observe yourself as you listen. As the other is speaking, relax your body and pay attention. Notice any habitual body movements, language, or sensations that arise within you. If you cross your arms in front of your chest, take note and uncross them. Be open and receptive.

Watch your tendency to drift off, attempt to read the person's mind, distract yourself, or imagine what he (or she) is going to say next. Watch your impulse to interrupt or jump in when the person pauses to take a breath or collect his thoughts. You might only hear what you expect to hear, rather than the actual words of what he is saying. You might notice that you have an initial judgment or interpretation, or that you label what he's saying and dismiss it. Be easy on yourself, but do notice these things and keep returning your focus to who's speaking.

As you listen, drop your awareness into your heart center, as you did in the *Heart-Centered Breath,* and listen from that perspective. Keep your attention on the present moment. His words might trigger thoughts about the past or future. When you notice that you aren't being present, come back and give him your attention once again. Get comfortable with the silence—his as well as your own. There is nothing you need to do or say. Simply be present and receive the communication as if you were in council and that person is holding the talking stick. Be sweet to yourself and completely present for him.

Schedule of Practices and Exercises

Week Six: Suggested Daily Practices	
AM	Heart-Centered Breath: 2 Minutes
	Self-Inquiry: Who Am I?: 3 Minutes
	Mantra or Sitting Meditation: 10 Minutes
PM	Mantra or Sitting Meditation: 15 Minutes

Additional Awareness Exercises	
Anytime	Listening with Love

Insights for Success

When you practice *Heart-Centered Breath, Self-Inquiry: Who Am I?* and your sitting meditations, you cultivate greater self-awareness and awareness of your own soul. Practice listening to your internal guidance system, your intuition, to make more nourishing choices; paying attention to your yeses and nos; and expressing yourself with integrity when faced with a choice. You honor yourself and everyone else by communicating honestly, saying what you mean, speaking your truth, and asking for what you want. Such honesty will create a security in your own wisdom, and with practice you'll feel more confident expressing yourself.

Practice being "in circle" with those you care about. Use some of the guidelines from the council practice as a guide to being present with others and yourself while you communicate. Notice when you feel moved to speak and share what you feel—resist the urge to hold it down. Learn to be comfortable with silence in communication. If you feel inspired, start your own communication circle or council practice with friends. Remember, honest communication with yourself and others is essential for a soul-centered life.

o o o

RECEPTIVITY: LOOK FOR WHAT MATTERS

*"Whatever the soul knows how
to seek, it cannot fail to obtain."*

— MARGARET FULLER, AMERICA'S FIRST FEMALE FOREIGN
CORRESPONDENT, HUMAN-RIGHTS ADVOCATE

By now, you've been paying attention to where you focus your attention, not only in meditation but in your life—and your life is transforming! Last week your focus was on your connection to your intuition and making choices aligned with it. You learned to honor yourself by listening to yourself and expressing your truth in your speech and actions. You also learned that being present while listening to someone is a wonderful way to honor another person. The *Heart-Centered Breath* enlivened your awareness of your own heart—it's a fantastic way to begin any meditation practice or even a conversation!

This week as you continue to hone your attention through your practice, focus on attending to your desires, of asking yourself what you want and acknowledging that. Attending to what is important to you and being open to receiving it with gratitude are essential to welcoming more of what you want into your life.

There's a basic principle I've found to be true: Life always meets your desires. This week, you'll learn how to have an ongoing dialogue with the universal source, that intelligent field of consciousness, the "one" that Emerson talked about. You'll learn to tap into its creativity, as it's the infinite organizing power that turns desires into reality. This field is the unseen, dynamic, creative, benevolent, infinite, and powerful source of all manifestation and creation in the universe—and it's on your side, supporting you.

Wanting What You Want

What do you want, really? Do you dare answer that question, even silently to yourself? When I ask my students what they really want, some of them have difficulty answering the question. One woman responded that she hadn't thought about it before. Perhaps she thought it selfish or sinful to want something for herself. Although she clearly knew what her husband, her kids, her grandkids, and even her neighbors wanted, her own desires were a mystery to her. (I could completely understand.) Another student answered, "World peace." Perhaps it was true, but often such abstractions, as worthy as they are, keep us from deeply asking our own soul what we *truly* want.

When I was first starting meditation, it wasn't easy for me to ask myself that question—never mind answering it! I believed it was more spiritual not to have any desires, so I tried not to. I ignored them. When any desires did arise, I didn't admit them, not even to myself.

My inquiry into what I wanted in life began one day during a group meditation. Deepak Chopra led it and suggested each one of us silently ask ourselves, "What is my heart's desire?" before we started meditating. Reluctantly, I asked myself the question, but I didn't have an answer. Instead, other questions came up for me: *Isn't it selfish to want something? Shouldn't I try to get rid of my desires? Aren't they selfish? Isn't the spiritual life more about world peace or being compassionate?*

I again focused on his instruction. I'd never before seriously asked myself the question he was posing. When asked specifically in the past, "What do you want, Sarah?" I didn't have a heartfelt, original, authentic answer. Mostly, I would scan the environment and the people in it for clues as to what answer might please others. Deepak had given me permission to ask myself the question, then be silent and listen. I did this, but initially only more doubts and confusion arose. I often knew what I *didn't* want when it presented itself . . . but what *did* I want?

Attention and Detachment

In my studies of Buddhism, I'd gotten the impression (wrongly) that the Buddha taught that desire was the cause of all suffering. Believing this was so, I'd made up my mind to not have any desires—as if that were even possible!—and thought that I was being spiritual by doing so. I later learned the Buddha actually taught that it's the *attachment* or clinging to desires that causes suffering, not the desires themselves. It made sense; how could I not have desires?

Obviously, I had all kinds of desires: I was always wanting something, whether it was a good meal, a parking space, a car that ran well, a fulfilling career, nurturing relationships, a safe environment, enough money to pay my bills, or peace on Earth. I also wanted a simple and happy life, I wanted a loving and nurturing relationship, I wanted to feel confident, I wanted to keep exploring mind-body healing, I wanted to travel the world, I wanted to be healthy, and I wanted to continue to be in a community of a spiritual nature. But at the time, I hadn't been *conscious* of these desires—they mostly had remained unacknowledged up until then.

Eventually I began to understand that desires are naturally part of who we are as human beings. We all have them—they are part of the software of our soul. It's what we do with them that can be a challenge, and where the suffering can come in. Do we cling to them or attach to them? Do we become controlling when we want to get what we want? Basically we are born with desires, and they couldn't be more natural. They lead us to take action, and these actions lead to memories, and then memories can inform our desires. We all have desires, and they are there to point us in the direction of a fulfilling life.

I continued to ask myself, "What do I want?" after that group meditation. I've noticed that if you ask a question, you will inevitably hear a response—the answer always meets the question. It may not come right away, or even when you want it, but there will be a response. Patience is key. Recall the questions I asked you in the Introduction: *What is my intention? How do I want to live my life? How do I want my life to transform?*

Over the next few weeks and months, I paid close attention. Eventually, I heard answers to my question . . . *lots* of answers. My desires were abundant, and I was embarrassed at first by how many of them came up, judging myself for what seemed like fantasizing too much. My internal dialogue echoed a voice from my past: "Quit being so selfish! Can't you think of someone besides yourself?" At the time, truthfully, the answer was no.

The desires came like waves. They came at all times: in the early morning when I was just waking up, as I went for a hike, in the shower, when I was driving my car. Many of them seemed impossible to fulfill, and paying attention to them seemed like an exercise in frustration. But it wasn't as stressful as not admitting to them. When my desires went unrecognized, they gnawed away at me and kept me from being at peace, and, ultimately, from living a fulfilling life. It was actually more honest to admit that I had them, and even less stressful.

During one meditation at the Zen Center, the desires seemed to accompany some energy that traveled up my spine. I was supposed to be sitting in meditation paying attention to my breath, but the feeling was so strong it was difficult to ignore. I felt the desire to be in a loving relationship with someone who understood my passions, beliefs, and values. There was the desire to live near the wilderness and to feel nourished by nature, to meditate regularly, and to maintain a serene inner being. I wanted to teach others to meditate and share what had been so instrumental in my own transformation. I wanted to be completely supported while doing it.

I refocused on my meditation practice, dismissing what I thought were ridiculous thoughts. When I stopped meditating that day, they returned. Since I didn't think there was much of a chance of ever realizing those dreams, I was truly unattached to them. Though I acknowledged them, on some level, I assumed the key to the fulfillment of these desires was to stay at the Zen Center for the rest of my life and hope for the best. It was in the wilderness, and it was a place I could meditate regularly and maintain serenity, while occasionally teaching.

As I acknowledged my desires, my life began to totally transform and my desires took shape. A few years later, I was living a life I had formerly only dreamed about—teaching meditation full-time and living at the edge of the high desert wilderness with my fiancé, Marty, in Sedona. Not only was I doing what I loved, but I had found someone who totally "got" me, someone I could share my life with. He's such a perfect match for me, I wouldn't even have been able to dream him up!

The manifestation of my desires did not unfold in a linear fashion, in a predictable time frame, or because of a particular goal-setting formula. It was a completely roundabout, organic path, created by making one intuitive choice after another. I knew what I wanted, and sometimes why I wanted it, but I had to leave the "how, when, and who" up to the creative intelligence, the source of all things. I had to surrender to life, not struggle against it, and welcome what it brought me while continuing to pay attention to my intentions without any attachment to them. No effort was involved; no force was required to make anything happen. The only requirement was paying attention, some practice, and a little faith.

How does this process work, having a desire or intention and then seeing the manifestation? Although there isn't a formula for achieving happiness, there are ingredients which I'd like to share with you here.

First allow yourself to ask the question, "What do I want?" Wait and listen. Be patient, and when your desires make themselves known, allow yourself to admit and acknowledge them, even writing them down if you like. Then, before you meditate, review those desires in your mind, letting go of any expectations about how they should happen. Sit in your meditation (one of the silent ones you have been learning) without further focus on what you want. When the meditation is over, don't expect anything. Instead of planning, follow your internal guidance system, making one conscious choice after another in response to whatever arises. It's a creative path, and follows no obvious order.

Consider the fact that your desires are fulfilled because inherent in the desire itself is the information necessary for its creation. *In-formation.* Desires take form. Desire is like a seed that has the potential to grow into something. It's the doorway between the potential of *what can be* and the reality of *what is.*

Let's use a cypress tree as an example. Every bit of intelligence needed to create another cypress tree—all the information for when and how to grow, thrive, and mature—can be found in the seed of this tree. All that is needed for the seed to germinate and grow is the attention or nourishment from the elements, the rain, sunshine, earth, air, and space. Analogously, your desire is the seed and your attention is the nourishment. You don't need to know how or when it will manifest; you simply need to plant your desire in this field of consciousness from which all things arise. Then nature's law takes over.

Quantum physics says that all things, at the most basic level, are made up of energy and information. That includes the manifestation of your desires. You shine your light of awareness (energy) on the seeds of your desire (information), and someday, something will germinate and grow. Your desires are meant to grow into fruition. And nature supports that.

A Meditator's Story:
Although It Seems like a Dream

Carol was a teacher at an inner-city school in Detroit. She had always been on a spiritual search, but began to pay more attention during a trip to Amsterdam one summer. She had made up her mind that she and her husband were going to retire there someday, so she took this opportunity to explore. In a travel book, she saw a listing for an Ayurvedic massage described as "two hours of bliss." She recognized the word *Ayurveda* from a book she'd been studying, Deepak Chopra's *Perfect Health,* and made her appointment.

When she arrived at the narrow row house, she was greeted with a cup of warm water, a traditional Ayurvedic beverage. After a healing oil massage, Carol left feeling totally blissful and energized. Eric, her husband, went to get a massage and also left grinning from ear to ear. Carol decided to further investigate Ayurveda when she got back to Michigan.

One day, Eric had a stroke and was in a coma for six weeks. When he came out of his coma, he was unable to speak, walk, or take care of himself. Then he began having seizures. Carol hated leaving him with an aide to go off to work, but felt she had to—there were only two years left before she could retire with benefits after a 30-year teaching career. A year later, Eric was still paralyzed on one side and having seizures, though they found a yoga teacher who was able to help him deal with his physical changes. Although their dream of retiring and moving to Amsterdam was dashed, Carol couldn't wait to retire so she could help with Eric's rehabilitation.

When winter came to Detroit that year, they knew they needed to get away to somewhere warm. They decided on Sedona without knowing much about it except that the climate was right. When they arrived, Carol realized that she had been there before, and Eric loved it instantly—they both felt a sense of peace. *This might work for us,* she thought, and they stayed a few weeks. When they went home, they both missed the peace and spirituality they felt in Sedona. So they returned later that year, and Carol decided to look for a meditation teacher. She found me.

Carol learned to meditate in one of my all-day classes. She told me that she wanted to move to Sedona but couldn't see a way. I told her to pay attention to her desire, let go of how it was going to happen, and keep on meditating. A week later, Eric joined the class to learn to meditate, too. They had both adopted regular meditation practices by the time they returned to Detroit and decided to sell their house. The couple returned to Sedona for yet another visit to attend a meditation retreat. They also began looking at houses (even though their home in Detroit hadn't sold yet), but didn't find one they liked. "I began to believe what I wanted could and would happen, someway, somehow," Carol said.

One day while back in Detroit and browsing the Internet, Carol found the house she was looking for. She called her agent in Arizona who said it was a good deal, and they bought it sight unseen. Carol called the bank to see if she could make an arrangement for the home in Detroit, but there was no negotiating with them. So they boarded up their house, left the keys with their agent, and left. She felt like she was escaping: first from the school system as she retired, and then from Detroit itself!

Carol's friends were surprised she was able to relocate so spontaneously, but Carol wasn't. She said, "I learned from meditating that anything I want is within reach, and that if I put out an intention, the universe will provide in ways I can't always foresee. I don't worry so much anymore. My intention is like writing a check, and the universe manages to cash it in.

"My blood pressure, which has always been high, has dropped since I've been out of Detroit. And the seizures Eric was experiencing have completely stopped since we've been here. Lots of new opportunities present themselves here, and when they feel good in my body, I say yes! That's how I know what to do next. Everything just shows up before I even know I need it. I now feel everything I do—whether finding a job, a meditation teacher, or a new house—is a form of meditation, and in general, I'm more content and at peace. I'm living the life I want to live."

Desires and Destiny

Sometimes we know what we want but our focus becomes *how* we're going to get it, and we lose sight of what we truly want. For instance, take the case of a young pregnant woman who came to me to learn to meditate. When I asked her what it was she truly wanted, she responded, "I want $200,000." I asked her what she planned to do with the money. "I'd buy a two-bedroom condo." She and her husband were currently living in a one-bedroom condo, and it definitely looked like they'd need the extra space with a new baby.

She knew *what* she wanted: space, peace, comfort, and joy; even another room in a bigger condo. But instead of keeping her attention on her actual desires, she skipped right to *how* to make them happen, determining the way in which it would unfold. This made her focus on a large sum of money she wanted. By focusing on the how, she limited the ways in which her desire could be met. There are many ways to get more space, but you never know *how* it will manifest; sometimes it is way beyond your wildest dreams. Why limit the possibilities?

If you find your desires are focused on having more money, ask yourself what you would do with it if you got it. You have the desire for something you think you can obtain with the money. Is it freedom? More time with the family? A new house? More space? Happiness? Remember that money is simply a means to an end— not the end itself. What do you really want?

○ ○

It's important to note that desires that arise are not random or accidental. It's said that you are born with certain programming, a certain set of desires, which are the cues to lead you to your destiny and purpose in life. Desires are not always personal, nor do they exist only for your own benefit; but rather, desires you have can exist for the good of all. They are part of the orchestration of the intelligent field of awareness. Desires are how the field expresses itself and creates reality—*through you.* This is expressed beautifully in a passage in the Upanishads, a sacred text from ancient India: "You are what your deep driving desire is. As your desire is, so is your will. As your will is, so is your deed. As your deed is, so is your destiny."

Desire and destiny—it all starts with you asking yourself what you want, and then being willing to hang in there and await the response. Meditation trains you to be more self-aware, focused, patient, and a better listener. So when you discover what you want, pay attention to your desires before you meditate. When you are in meditation and activity, let go of all attachment as to how your desires will come to fruition, the same way you let go of the outcome of your practice. Let your focus be in the moment you're in, exactly how it is.

With your attention in the present, you have the opportunity to pay attention to clues in your environment, as well as to tune in and use your internal guidance system to navigate life's many choices. Don't keep your focus on the future, waiting for something to happen—that would keep you in perpetual wishing, longing, and ultimately suffering when things don't go as you planned. Instead, practice accepting and even appreciating "what is" right now. When your attention is in the present moment, you'll be attentive when your desires have been made manifest!

Understandably, there's often discomfort that accompanies such uncertainty and the unknown. Consider, however, that in reality, nothing is truly certain except this moment. Questions such as "When will it happen?" "Who will it be?" "Where will I go?" and "How will it work?" often accompany desires. To keep the discomfort and suffering to a minimum, it is important to have faith in the universal intelligence and leave the specifics up to it.

You might have heard the phrase, "Let go and let God." This applies here. Let the universe handle the details; you don't have to micromanage a thing. You will soon realize that desires and attention activate a very real law of nature. As your desires become reality, it will cultivate more faith in the intelligent field to orchestrate a perfect unfoldment. The universe will keep fulfilling your desires to give you what you want until there's a natural shift, and you find yourself wanting and appreciating what the universe has already given you—you want what you already have!

Being Open to Receive

It is one thing to get in touch with your desires and know what you want, but it is an entirely different thing to be open to receiving what the universe brings in response. The ability to be "open to receive" is just as important as understanding your desire or intention. Think of what would happen and how you'd feel if you gratefully received all that was offered to you: a sunrise, a cool breeze, someone's smile, or even a traffic jam or speeding ticket. Welcoming and receiving each and every moment, whatever it brings, is a great way to go through life.

Personally, I find it harder to receive than to give. When I give, I often feel more comfortable because I am in control. Receiving means that I must surrender to and welcome the gifts that are coming toward me, whatever they may be. To that end, as an adult, I hadn't let myself be taken care of by another, not physically, emotionally, or financially. Most of my life I'd been the one doing the giving, even making it a point of pride to think of myself as fully independent and self-sufficient. I supported myself—and, in my co-dependent style, often supported my partners by buying the groceries, paying the rent, going into debt for this or that. All that shifted when I decided to be kind to myself.

After Marty proposed to me, I moved to Sedona. My savings kept me afloat for the first few months, but those funds dwindled quickly. The bills kept coming, and it was getting difficult to pay them. One afternoon, Marty asked me how I was doing. He had a sense that I was a little disturbed. The thought of revealing my situation made me feel as if I were a bad, irresponsible person. I felt ashamed as I told him I was trying to figure out how to pay a couple of bills. It was a big deal for me to admit that I couldn't do it on my own. I tended to not let myself be vulnerable, and I hid the parts of myself that were scared and in need. But I had made a commitment to reveal all of me, as it arose. I was engaged, and that meant showing up in this relationship authentically.

Marty understood and asked to see the bills. He laid them out on the dining room table, got his checkbook, and started writing checks without a word. He wrote one for each of my bills, including entirely paying off a long-lingering college loan. What a relief! I cried when he did it, and I'm even crying now just thinking of it. It was such a release from the years of maintaining this self-sufficient façade, suppressing even the urge to ask for help.

Receiving help was very unfamiliar to me, but that afternoon I learned a new practice: how to receive what is given. This is a necessary ingredient to having your desires met and living a fulfilling life. Receiving is different from taking, because receiving is part of the circle of giving. One can't give without another to receive, just as one can't receive without the giving. This week is all about becoming more receptive and welcoming to what is offered.

For most of us, receiving is something we need to practice. You've already gotten a good start with your present-moment-awareness practices. You must be aware of the moment in order to receive it! Then, as you've been doing in meditation, practice receiving sounds, sensations, and silence. Practice receiving guidance from intuition, receiving your emotions and how your body feels. Practice receiving your desires, inspiration, and creativity. Practice receiving compliments, kindnesses, and service from others. Practice receiving everything in life that supports you, whether it's air, water, fire, space, earth, sounds, sensations, sights, smells, tastes, plants, animals, beauty, food, health, relationships, companionship, money, or employment.

Receiving all that is given to you in each moment helps create a welcoming attitude to all that is. You can even practice receiving pain, illness, and death. As Steve Jobs, the co-founder of Apple, lay dying, surrounded by his family, his final words illustrated his welcoming attitude toward what was happening: "Oh wow. Oh wow. Oh wow." That's what I call being open to the universe— and whatever it may bring.

Appreciating Your Life

Welcoming and appreciating what is here right now is essential to fulfilling your desires. No matter what your feelings are about having desires, your world is always better when you appreciate your life and all that supports you in the moment. "I love my life." "I appreciate my life." Say those words to yourself and truly feel them. Feeling grateful is a sweet sensation. When you feel grateful, your mind is clear, you have a relationship to the universe and its creator, and you become more aware of the big picture. Gratitude refines your focus and sensitivity and helps direct your focus to the good things in life.

There's science that backs this up. Research on gratitude has shown that grateful people have lower levels of stress and depression; and they experience more vitality, optimism, and higher levels of positive emotions. They have a greater capacity for empathy and are viewed as more generous and more helpful by others. People who appreciate their lives see the interconnectedness of life and have a sense of responsibility and commitment to others. Also, grateful people place less importance on their own material wealth and are less likely to judge others based on what they have. They are also more likely to share what they have with those who don't have as much. In general, they are more satisfied with life.

Dr. Robert Emmons of the University of California, Davis, says that those who learn to be grateful can experience the world as a friendly place. It even creates a spiritual awakening for some people as they realize each moment of their life is a gift. He and Dr. Michael McCullough of the University of Miami have been conducting ongoing research on gratitude and thankfulness. They found that people who keep weekly gratitude journals feel better about their lives on the whole and are more optimistic about the future compared to those who didn't keep gratitude journals.

You can experiment with this in your own life, too. A gratitude journal is simply a notebook where you write a list of people, things, or experiences you are grateful for. So take a minute or two every day to write a list of a few things you are grateful for, and be specific. You can do it every night before bed, or first thing in the morning right before you meditate. You might even make your list mentally.

At times, it can be easy to come up with the list; at other times, you may find it hard to think of even two things. That's when you could remember how amazing it is that your heart has been beating since before you were born, that you're able to breathe and move, and that you can experience this world with your senses. You might acknowledge all the people, places, and things that have contributed to your life and supported you. Think of your parents and their parents and so on. As the Chinese proverb says, "When eating bamboo sprouts, remember the man who planted them."

Perhaps being appreciative will come spontaneously. You'll notice the way the clouds form in the sky, or the way the sunlight reflects off the leaves of a tree; and instead of ignoring it, you'll acknowledge it, appreciate it, and receive it. You can include all things in your gratitude. Every moment is an opportunity to appreciate your life. But some of us need cues to remember. I remember to say "Thank you" when I first awaken—it sets the day for me. Every meal is also an opportunity to appreciate and receive. What will you use as your own cues?

Although it is sometimes challenging to cultivate the attitude of gratitude in the midst of a difficult situation, or when wanting something you don't have, it is essential. It's impossible to be grateful and in fear at the same time. When life is difficult and you feel great sorrow or anxiety, or if you're dealing with a difficult relationship, choosing to be grateful can transform your perspective—even if it's only for a few moments—to one of appreciation and contentment for all that is, both the wonderful and the frustrating.

When you feel grateful, your brain produces endorphins, which are the same chemicals that reduce stress, lessen pain, and improve your immune functions. You become more comfortable with accepting each moment as it is, knowing that ultimately everything is happening for your own evolution. When you look for good things, you begin to expect good things, and this expectation becomes faith. Being grateful puts you in a totally different mind-set and energy level, enabling you to reestablish your connection to your soul center.

The Power of Attention

Have you seen the video that asks you to count how many times students throw and catch a basketball? It's part of a study on selective attention. For just over a minute, the video shows a basketball being passed around on the court from player to player. Once it's over, another question is asked, "But did you see the gorilla?" I thought, *Gorilla? What gorilla?* I hadn't been looking for *that.* I was counting and completely missed the person in the gorilla suit waltzing across the screen in between the players throwing the ball. (I saw it clearly when I rewatched the video.) At least I wasn't alone! According to one study, half the people tested didn't notice the gorilla, either. And they were as shocked as I was when asked about it. This is because most people think they'd see something as obvious as a gorilla walking through a basketball game. This study illustrates how much we overestimate our ability to accurately see one thing when we are focused on something else; focus is that powerful.

My friend Mary's story also demonstrates the power of attention. She told me, "Yesterday I decided to make fragrant herbal tea. I set a big pot on the stove, added the tea, set the timer for 22 minutes, and went into another room to read a novel. When the timer went off, I looked up from my book and immediately smelled the sweet tea. What struck me is that I didn't smell the tea until after the timer beeped. Think of it—was the fragrance in the air before the timer went off? Of course it was. But because my attention was elsewhere, I didn't notice it. In my world, it didn't exist. Our focus impacts our perception of reality. There are opportunities right under our noses every day, but because of a simple lack of focus, they can go completely unnoticed." I think she'd like the gorilla video.

If you aren't looking for something, you likely won't find it. The opposite can also be true. Once something catches your eye, you begin to see it everywhere. Whatever you are looking for is enlivened in your awareness—it's all a matter of perspective and attention. So, be conscious of what you want to see or hear or experience. Make sure it's really what you want.

○ ○

I discovered for myself that what you look for is what you get, and this awareness led me to make a different choice in my life.

One hot summer day, Marty and I were driving through the streets of Phoenix. As usual, I kept my eyes peeled, on the look-out for signs of animals big or small that might be hot, hungry, thirsty, neglected, or needing help of some kind. I can tend toward being a compulsive animal rescuer. I looked everywhere: between buildings, through fences, into apartment windows, on stairwells, and in corrals.

As we drove along, my eyes darting in my search, I became aware of an overall bodily discomfort. I was holding my breath, I felt anxious, and my chest was tight—things that I might not have noticed if my usual state wasn't calm and restful from all my years of meditation. One thing was sure, I wasn't having fun. A great song might have been playing on the radio, but I wasn't listening. A beautiful wildflower might have been blooming, but I couldn't see it. Nothing else mattered in the moment.

I began to think about a trip I'd taken one weekend with my 11-year-old niece, Courtney, to New York City. As we were walking together down a busy street near Times Square, she announced to me that everyone in New York was "mean." I asked her how she knew that, and she assured me that she could tell. "Their faces *look* mean," she said, pointing at the sour expressions on the faces of a few passersby. I hadn't been seeing it that way, and I offered her a chance to see things differently by doing a simple exercise. She agreed.

I asked her to stop for a moment and look around to find everything around her that was the color blue. She didn't need to tell me what she saw; I wanted her to simply take note. She scanned the storefronts and people on that street for anything blue, and signaled me when she felt complete. Then I asked her to close her eyes and tell me of anything she'd seen that was *red*. She kept her eyes closed and was silent. She couldn't recall a single red thing. After all, red hadn't been what she was looking for!

Courtney opened her eyes. I told her that the mind usually finds what it's looking for and little else. Once you have a thought about the way things are, the mind finds anything to provide you with evidence so you can be right. I asked her, "Is it possible you didn't see some of the kinder faces once you decided people were mean?" She shrugged as if to concede my point, and she had a little more fun as we continued down the block.

As Marty and I drove along that hot day, I realized that my looking for suffering animals was similar to my niece's seeing "mean" people everywhere. Habits are strong, but with awareness, it's always possible to make another choice as to how to respond. So I decided I would look for something else—the red instead of the blue. I would consciously look for *beauty* instead of animals suffering. I decided beauty could be in any form, shape, or experience. I wanted to see the beauty I knew existed.

Immediately, my eyes lit on a sign that read BEAUTY. I laughed. It was a beauty-supply shop! I continued to look, and beauty showed up everywhere—in the color of the buildings, in the clouds in the sky, in the music on the radio, in the glimmer of the sunlight and the shadows it cast on the desert landscape as we drove.

Did the shift in my awareness from pain to beauty cause me to forget or ignore those in need? No. Did animals stop suffering? No. Although I was no longer on the lookout for pain and suffering, I would still passionately respond to such a situation. But I chose instead to have a more expanded awareness, and it made my trip more enjoyable and my body more relaxed. Now I continue to be on the lookout for how to help, but it's from a peaceful, holistic, and relaxed perspective that is much more enjoyable and healthy.

I am also still looking for and finding beauty. My search reminds me of this Native American chant used in ceremonies to encourage our return to a state of balance with creation. The state of balance is called *hozho* in the Navajo language, and the chant goes like this:

In beauty I walk
With beauty before me, I walk
With beauty behind me, I walk
With beauty below me, I walk
With beauty above me, I walk
With beauty all around me, I walk
It is finished in beauty

Practices and Exercises to Cultivate Receptivity

Embodying Your Beauty

Looking for what is important to us is a powerful way of paying attention. What you look for will be enlivened in your awareness, including qualities in people we admire. Often we don't even realize that we have them, too; but if we look for them in others, we can find them in ourselves. This practice is about enlivening qualities in yourself that you admire in others.

First, make a short list of four or five people you admire. The list can include those who are alive or dead, mythical or real. It could include your mom, your grandfather, your first-grade teacher, a biblical figure, or a world leader.

Alongside each name identify four or five attributes you admire about each one of them. These attributes could include things like how they act or how they treat others, how they look or present themselves, the choices they make, and the jobs they do.

Next, bring your attention to yourself. Go through the list and for each attribute you've written down, find the ways in which you already embody that same quality. Take your time; sit with it like a meditation. It might take a moment, but you will eventually discover that you do, even if only in your thoughts, have those same qualities that you admire in another. What you put your attention on grows, and what you admire in others are qualities you can discover, embody, and express in your own life. Once you do this exercise, continue to keep your focus on these qualities, especially ones that are harder to own, and look for opportunities to express them. You might surprise yourself!

Gratitude Meditation

You don't have to feel grateful to do this meditation; instead, it's designed to generate a feeling of gratitude and appreciation, regardless of how you feel now. Practicing gratitude is helpful even when you are in a difficult situation.

This practice is good to do at any time, for as long as you like. You can do it on its own or in conjunction with *Sitting Meditation*. You can even practice it as you lie in bed before sleep.

Here's what to do:

— Find a quiet, comfortable spot where you will not be disturbed. Sit or lie down in a comfortable position. Close your eyes and be still.

— Allow the stress and tension to fade away as you scan and relax your body from head to toe: your face, your shoulders, your belly, your arms, your legs, and so on.

— Pay attention to your breath, feeling it as it comes and goes, in and out of your body. Imagine that your breath is moving into and out of your heart center.

— Take slow, easy, deep breaths through your nose. Allow your lungs to fill completely with air. Feel the breath right down to your tailbone. Hold the inhale for the count of three, then let go. Hold the exhale for the count of three, then let go. Let the breath return to its natural rhythm.

167

— Shift your attention to your heart-centered breath; if it's easy for you, imagine the entire heart area filling with light for a few moments.

— Next, bring your attention to what you feel grateful for in your life. Begin with your own life: you can start with the basics. You can appreciate your breath or being alive or the abundance and support of nature that feeds your body and soul. Maybe you feel grateful for your work, your talent and passions, your home, or your environment. Whatever occurs to you, go with that.

— Bring your attention to people who truly nourish you in your life. Appreciate how they bless you with their presence.

— Next, appreciate the qualities of your own soul: your creativity, awareness, expansiveness, wisdom, timelessness, love, stability, flexibility, purity, spaciousness, freedom, etc.

— Next, appreciate the qualities as they apply to your life. For instance, when you think of freedom, you can appreciate the freedom that is inherently yours, your freedoms of thought, choice, and speech. You have the freedom to live your life the way you choose, to imagine, to create.

— Let your appreciation embrace all creation and life itself, with all its beauty and diversity. Include the universe, the creative intelligence, the divine presence in your life, and the interconnection of all things. Add anything else that you are grateful for, or simply pay attention to how you are feeling and the sensations in your body.

— Again, bring your attention on your heart center, and silently repeat the words, *Thank you.*

— When you feel complete, give yourself a few long, slow, deep breaths and sit or lie in the stillness.

— Slowly open your eyes, first with a downward gaze. Notice how you feel. Wait until you feel ready to fully open your eyes. Take your time getting up.

Self-Inquiry: What Is My Heart's Desire?

This inquiry is for you, whether you know what you really desire or not. Don't worry if you don't know what you want. Ask, and the answers will come to you eventually. When you put your attention on your intention before you meditate, even if the intention is to discover your desires, you sow seeds for its manifestation.

You can do this practice anytime and anywhere, sitting up or lying down. I prefer to do it sitting up and before I go into my meditation period. Remember to do this practice with a beginner's mind. Here's how to begin:

— Find a comfortable position. Close your eyes and relax your body.

— Bring your attention to your heart center; focus your breath on your heart. Let your breathing be soft and normal.

— With your focus on your heart, ask yourself, "What do I really want? What is my heart's desire?"

— Wait a few moments and listen. Don't try to answer the questions by thinking of what you want or by making something up because you think it's the right thing to want.

— Be authentic. Wait, listening in the silence. You may or may not hear an answer right away. The desires will arise in their own time now that you have given yourself permission to want something.

— If you already know what you want, then you can gently bring your attention to those desires in your mind and heart. If you don't know what you want yet, however, simply sit quietly with the question.

— Do not get into a story of how, when, who, or where it will manifest. Let go of any aversions, too—those thoughts of what you don't want. Simply pay attention to *what* you desire. Detach from the outcome of this process. Do this for a few minutes before opening your eyes slowly.

Walking in a Wonderful World

This week, go for a walk in a wonderful world. If you are struggling with a decision, or have a particular dilemma or situation you want insight into, you can do this practice with that in mind. You can do it whether you are walking in the wilderness or in a grocery-store parking lot; it will be effective either way.

Begin by relaxing your body, and take some deep breaths as you stand still. Bring your question or issue to mind. Bring your full attention to it before you begin your walk. Then, let it go.

As you walk, simply receive everything that you experience, sense by sense, as if everything that meets your senses is a gift for you. Receive the breeze as it slips past your skin, receive the solidity of the ground as it meets each step, enjoy the fragrances that are offered, and feel the sun's warmth. The sky is offering you its clouds, sun, and blueness; the birds serenade you. Any sound is for you to enjoy, and if you don't enjoy it, perhaps you enjoy the silence it leaves.

If you look, everything in nature is very wise, offering you an answer, a lesson, or a gift you could benefit from. Everything is for you. See what insights you might have. Maybe you simply feel loved and supported. Imagine: it's *all* for you to receive. So, receive it. Walking in this way will assure you that it's a friendly world.

Schedule of Practices and Exercises

Week Seven: Suggested Daily Practices	
AM	Heart-Centered Breath: 2 Minutes Self-Inquiry: What is My Heart's Desire?: 3 Minutes Mantra or Sitting Meditation: 10 Minutes
PM	Mantra or Sitting Meditation: 15 Minutes

Additional Awareness Exercises	
Anytime	Gratitude Meditation Embodying Your Beauty Walking in a Wonderful World

Insights for Success

In the beginning of the program, you were asked to identify your reasons for going on this journey. With each meditation you've engaged in, your intentions were present on some level each time you sat down to practice. The practices this week revolve around wanting what you want, welcoming what is present, saying "yes" to receiving, saying "thank you" as you identify and appreciate what you already have, and noticing what you pay attention to.

Doing the *Self-Inquiry: What Is My Heart's Desire?* helps you identify or confirm what it is you truly want. *Walking in a Wonderful World* and the *Gratitude Meditation* help you stabilize this attitude of welcoming all that is and appreciating what you've already been blessed with in this life. These two practices are complementary to the sitting meditations (which you should continue to practice for a total of 30 minutes every day).

While you practice the *Gratitude Meditation* or the *Self-Inquiry,* focus on the practice at hand. While practicing the *Sitting* or *Mantra Meditation,* simply focus on the breath or mantra. Don't switch around your techniques in the middle of any practice; instead, train your attention steadily. Putting your attention on your desires or on what you're grateful for during a mantra or breath meditation can interfere with the natural process of the mind settling down. Do one thing at a time.

You are on an exciting journey! Follow your internal guidance system. Make choices in alignment with your truth. Look for what you want to experience more of. In your life and in meditation, continue to keep your attention in the present moment. This will help you be alert to the creative response from life, and to welcome it as it meets your desires. Trust that all will unfold perfectly in the right time. Presence, intuition, gratitude, receptivity, and integrity are essential to living a soul-centered life.

○ ○ ○

NOURISHMENT: CONTINUE THE TRANSFORMATION

"Fear less, hope more. Eat less, chew more.
Whine less, breathe more. Talk less, say more.
Hate less, love more. And all good things are yours."

— SWEDISH PROVERB

It's the final week of this 8-week program to transform your life. You've been learning how to use your internal guidance system over the past weeks, which has been telling you what steps to take when guided by the sensations of your body, the whisperings of your intuition, and your yeses and nos. If you haven't already, you'll soon discover that following your inner knowing, coupled with present-moment awareness, is the way to create a fulfilling life. Good for you!

You have probably gained a host of benefits from your new meditation practice. Perhaps your health has improved, and you feel less stressed. You may have discovered your intuition, and don't feel so judgmental of yourself and others. I hope that you've enhanced your ability to be receptive and grateful. Good things are happening, and you will make lasting changes with continued practice. Remember the old adage, "Whatever you do every day is stronger medicine than whatever medicine you take occasionally," and keep up the good work!

Meditation will keep you on the right path of your soul-centered life, whether you want to be less stressed in your work; more present for your relationships; more radiant, authentic, and creative; or simply fulfilled by life. In addition to the practices you've learned in this program, this week you'll learn additional ways to nourish and support your body and mind. You'll discover shifts you can make in your daily routine to maximize your digestion and enhance the quality of your sleep to rejuvenate yourself.

Besides meditation, eating well, and sleeping soundly, another terrific way to nourish yourself is to choose one day a month for a retreat. You don't even need to leave home; instead, you can create your own mini–meditation retreat right where you live. The suggestions at the end of this chapter will help you stabilize that inner silence you're becoming more familiar with, so you can more easily get into the gap.

Early to Bed, Early to Rise

Do you know the best way to recover from stress? Perhaps you'd be surprised to hear that it's *not* meditation. Yes, meditation does give the body deep rest, and is the perfect antidote to the stress response. However, sleep is actually the number one way the body recovers from stress. A good night's sleep is the primary way your body rejuvenates and repairs itself, reduces stress levels, optimizes your immune system, and rebalances your hormone levels. Sleep improves memory, helps your body eliminate toxins efficiently, improves your mood, and naturally rejuvenates your body and mind.

Millions of people of all ages are affected by sleep problems, many with chronic sleep deprivation and severe sleep debt (which is a state of fatigue that accumulates over time). Between 1960 and 2010, the average night's sleep for adults in the U.S. dropped from more than 8 to 6.5 hours. More than 30 percent of adults say that they have some symptoms of insomnia within a given year, and 10 to 15 percent say they have chronic insomnia. According to an article in *The New York Times*, over 42 million sleeping-pill prescriptions were filled in 2005, up nearly 60 percent in five years. Sleep is a natural phenomenon, so no outside substances should be required for you to achieve a natural, rejuvenating rest. What is happening?

While we've all heard the pleas for eating right and exercising, we don't hear much about the importance of sleep. Sleep deprivation can lead to more than just feeling foggy in the morning. When you're tired, your brain performs less effectively, which leads to difficulty focusing and memory problems. Without enough sleep, your body limits the amount of energy it has, and this causes a variety of physical- and mental-health issues. Your immune system weakens, and the body becomes more vulnerable to infection and disease. Researchers have also found that getting a good night's sleep is imperative for normal, healthy aging.

Many of us choose to defer sleep in order to get things done, and plan on sleeping in later to "catch up." But we usually don't get enough extra rest to repay our sleep debt, and oftentimes this is because of stress. It's ironic that the mechanism the body uses to relieve stress gets interrupted because of that very same stress . . . causing more stress!

Normally, your level of the stress hormone cortisol spikes in the morning as you wake up, but otherwise it remains at low levels, especially in the beginning of the night's sleep. However, your daytime levels of cortisol rise whenever you're stressed, and this reduces the quality of your sleep. Fortunately, meditation reduces cortisol, thereby helping you get your sleeping patterns back on track.

Those who practice meditation say that as time goes by, the sleep they get is deeper and more refreshing, and they feel more alert and relaxed throughout the day. This claim has been supported by numerous studies. For instance, researchers at the University of Alberta, Canada, discovered that meditation reduces the effect of sleep disruptions caused by high levels of stress hormones. Insomnia sufferers who normally spent an average of 70 minutes awake before falling asleep began meditating every day. After 30 days, on average, they were able to fall asleep in just 15 minutes. A 1996 study of more than 100 people who suffered with chronic insomnia found that each and every patient who began a daily meditation practice reported improved sleep, with the majority reporting significant improvement. Of those meditators on sleep medicines, over 90 percent either eliminated or reduced their medication usage.

Another way to get good sleep is by following the axiom, "Early to bed, early to rise." Your body's circadian rhythms are very definite about when it's bedtime and when it's time to get up. However, these rhythms have been interrupted by modern-day conveniences such as electricity, which makes it easy to stay up as long as you want to work, shop, read, or whatever else you please.

In contrast, ancient wisdom decrees that the slower rhythm of the day kicks in at 6 P.M.; and most health experts agree that lights should be out around 10 P.M. to ensure proper rest. Staying up later puts you into a cycle that doesn't necessarily support falling asleep. Ideally, aim for six to eight hours of sleep. You can maximize your chances of falling asleep at night by arising around sunrise. Leave the window coverings open in your bedroom to let the early-morning sunlight reset your body's clock.

When your body is in balance, and you've reduced the effects of stress through meditation, you will wake up easily and naturally. Being well rested is an essential component of feeling soul-centered.

Perfect Health Through Perfect Digestion

One of the big jobs your body has to do every day is gain nourishment through food. As they say, "You are what you eat." You take in the outside world in the form of food, which your digestive system assimilates and turns into the stuff that makes up your body. It's no wonder that practitioners of Ayurveda say, "Perfect health is gained through perfect digestion."

What happens between your mouth and your stomach may be the first image that comes to mind when you think of digestion. However, the word *digestion* has many applications, including how you assimilate and extract nourishment from what you experience when you're experiencing it. Whether it's an ice cream sundae, a compliment from a friend, an emotional moment, a sweet embrace, or a stroll in the park, you digest it. As with food, what we don't fully digest in life can create toxicity in the body and mind. This is one of the reasons to practice being present—you have to be present to digest what is happening. If you aren't, it contributes to stress.

Let's get back to eating. There are so many theories on what is best to eat, so I won't go much into that. Instead, I offer you general guidelines based on ancient wisdom. Food, like any experience, can have an effect on your sense of contentment, so you want what you eat to be nourishing on all levels.

Each meal should be comprised of different textures, colors, and tastes. Ideally, your food should be in season, freshly prepared, wholesome, organic, and delicious. Eat that which is in its natural state, not processed. If you can, get locally grown produce. Don't overcook your food or eat too many leftovers. Reduce animal products and avoid genetically modified foods. Be mindful of what you put in your body, remembering that high-quality, organic, unprocessed foods contain more of nature's intelligence. The closer to its natural state the food is in, the more intact the nutrition.

How you eat is just as important to your health as what you eat. In Week Three, you practiced *Delectable Eating,* and you may have found that you better enjoyed what you ate when you slowed down and brought more awareness to the process. However, so many people's "food meditation" consists of cravings, drive-throughs, missing meals, and speed-eating.

Consider how you tend to eat. Do you just scarf things down on the go, while walking or driving? Do you even notice your food when you eat? While you're eating, I suggest that all you do is . . .

eat. Do one thing at a time. Always sit down to eat, and not in the car. Don't hang over the edge of the counter as you eat, or snack while doing dishes. Avoid eating while working or watching TV (especially disturbing programs or the news). Put down the book, get away from the computer, and get off the phone. Just eat!

If you want to have the best digestion, sit down while you eat, and do so in a quiet, relaxed atmosphere. Clear off the table and light some candles. Eat with people you enjoy pleasant conversation with, but don't talk while chewing your food. Avoid confrontations, serious discussions, or worry during meals, as this can compromise your digestion. If you feel stressed or upset, stop eating and relax for a bit before continuing with your meal. What you eat, how you cook, when you eat, who you eat with, and how you eat—these seemingly small choices have a big impact on your overall health, and ultimately on your longevity.

"Chew your drink, and drink your food" was the advice Gandhi gave for improving digestion. "Chewing your drink" refers to holding liquids in your mouth until they are the temperature of your body, so the liquids won't put out your digestive fire when you swallow. Avoid iced drinks with your meal, even though they love to serve them to you at restaurants. Politely say, "Please, no ice!"

"Drinking your food" means to chew very thoroughly, until the food is like liquid. It is similar to another wise saying that you might have heard, "Let your knife and fork do the work of your teeth, and let your teeth do the work of your stomach." Digestion begins in your mouth with a specific enzyme released in the saliva that is critical to the breakdown of carbohydrates. Without that enzyme, the other digestive enzymes in the small intestine and stomach won't work as efficiently. Your taste buds are also detecting what food you're eating so that the rest of your digestive system has the proper enzymes to break everything down. So chew, and chew carefully.

Chewing for a long time will slow you down, which is a good thing. Eating at a relaxed pace allows ample time to trigger the signal from your brain that you're full. It takes approximately

20 minutes from the time you start eating for your brain to send these signals. This is supported by a study in Japan involving 1,700 young women. The researchers found that eating more slowly resulted in feeling full sooner, and the women ate fewer calories overall, even reporting a greater feeling of satiation up to 60 minutes later.

Eat only when you're hungry *and* after your last meal has been fully digested (about two to six hours after a main meal). Don't eat just because it's mealtime or because everyone else is. When you follow the natural rhythms of nature, it's best to have your larger meal in the middle of the day when digestion is the strongest. Eat lightly for dinner, ideally before 7 P.M., because heavier meals at night can interfere with sleep. Take a walk after eating to enhance your digestion. And eat after your meditations, not before. These simple suggestions will help you improve your digestion and conserve your body's energy, but more important, they will also help you prevent toxicity and stress from accumulating in your body and mind.

A Meditator's Story: Living an Intentional Life

Victoria and I met when we were both new to Sedona. With our common interests of writing and meditating, we quickly became friends. I admired her perspective on life—she believed that life could be lived however you choose it.

Victoria grew up in the Dominican Republic, one of four children. She was a sensitive, wild, and independent child. Her best friend was a mango tree, and she trusted her intuition more than anything else. When she was 15, the family was deported from the D.R. and came to the U.S., with none of them speaking a word of English. Although they'd been an affluent family in their home country, in the U.S. they felt poor in comparison. They wanted the good life once again, and education and hard work were the keys her father identified as the way to realizing it. Victoria and her siblings took heed. One sister became an engineer, the other became a doctor, and her younger brother became a lawyer.

Victoria pursued her B.S. degree in economics. While in her last year at college, she married Peter, a man who was studying engineering at the same school. They had a similar vision for themselves: a simple, self-directed life. Victoria landed a job in the growing computer industry as a business-development manager, and Peter worked in the aerospace industry. They banked 50 percent of their annual income. The company Victoria was working for soon went public, and she was awarded IPO shares.

As she recalled, "Back then, I was a motivated and ambitious young woman, with no time for anything other than work—I hadn't known that I had that kind of earning potential and was completely hypnotized by it." Soon Victoria was locked into her high-paying job, and it required lots of travel and long hours. Her husband would say, "You're spending all of your time, youth, and energy on people you don't care about. You don't have time for me, your friends, or your family members." And he was right. Victoria put everyone who mattered to her on the back burner, thinking, *I'll get to them at some point.*

Then her mother was diagnosed with colon cancer and given three months to live. Victoria immediately took a leave of absence from her job to be with her. She didn't care whether her job would still be there when she returned, and spent weeks at a time caring for her mother. As she described it, "We sat in her room for hours in silence. Because of my profession, I hadn't been that still in years. When my mother spoke, it was often about what really mattered in her life; that I paid attention to what she said made her happy. She spoke of simple things—like us being together, eating a good meal, and feeling loved." Her mother's words reminded Victoria of the future she and Peter had envisioned together: to live a self-directed, simple life where the important things remained in the forefront. She no longer wanted to give her whole life away to her job.

Victoria's mother died five months later. Devastated, Victoria returned home. She returned to work with a plan to negotiate a new schedule: she wanted to work for only six months out of the year while still bringing in the same income for the company.

But management wouldn't hear of it. Instead, they wanted her to make up for the 16 weeks she was gone, and offered her a promotion and a raise to develop the Latin American market. Victoria was stubborn, and wanted what she wanted. They wouldn't say yes to her demands, but they wouldn't fire her either. She finally resigned after months of stalemate, without any plan except to simplify her life.

Victoria gave herself a year to grieve her mother and figure out what she would do next. She was being courted by myriad computer companies, each offering a great salary, but none allowing the schedule she wanted. She turned them all down. It was a turning point for her, choosing what mattered to her over what she thought she "should" be doing.

At first, she was lost without her old identity and hectic schedule. It was difficult just to get through the day. She said, "I needed to figure out who I was and what was important to me outside of my career role. My phone wasn't ringing anymore, I wasn't going to meetings, or flying off in airplanes. I had to figure out how to make a day make sense."

Gradually, she revisited the activities she'd loved doing before her career took off, turning to writing, cooking, bicycling, and studying philosophy. "I started doing things for my own happiness and health and stopped focusing on what society values. I could create a new life for myself around what I loved. I always said that I would teach myself to paint, and this was the perfect time to start."

Victoria and her husband bought a parcel of land located inside the national forest. Then they designed and built an environmentally friendly straw-bale home together. A few years later, Peter also left his job after being fully vested in his company. Their daily routine is now one of their own choosing—and they couldn't be happier.

A typical day for Victoria now starts with early-morning meditation, then a long walk in nature. "I get up when I've had enough sleep—a radical idea! And I don't answer my phone or e-mails until I'm ready to take a timed break. I paint, I write, I cook—when

I'm not doing that, I'm hanging out with my husband and other people I love."

While in college, Victoria had learned Transcendental Meditation, but like everything else, it went by the wayside when she pursued her career path. After moving to Sedona, she started meditating again and took a class with me. "Meditation helps me keep my attention on what matters in life," she told me. "If I get confused or off-track, I can still my mind long enough to find out what I really want." Victoria now knows that it takes intention and attention to pursue a fulfilling and peaceful life. "A daily meditation helps anyone have better focus," she reported. "Each day, each moment, you can choose what matters, what you want to focus on. Then when you keep your attention on it and make mindful choices, something great happens. You are like a train on a track, and ultimately, you get to your destination."

Unplug for a Day

The 8-week program in this book is about finding stillness and silence in meditation, but there's another way to bathe in silence: give yourself an entire day to unplug. This means unplugging from your electronics, from your responsibilities, from your roles, from your schedule, and from your ideas of what you should be doing. Unplug from interruptions and from noise—unplug from *everything*.

Abraham Lincoln learned to do this years ago. He was so often bothered by visitors in his office that he had little time to himself during the workday. At the end of his first term and in preparation for his second inaugural address, he began to sequester himself for four-hour periods of complete silence each day. He discovered that silence was essential for him to be clearer and more thoughtful.

Silence is also good for your health. Constant, low-level noise has a subtle yet insidious effect on your nervous system and health; it can create anxiety and nervousness. Even if you don't notice air traffic, road noise, or the hubbub at work, it doesn't mean you're unaffected by it. Studies show that children who live in noisy neighborhoods or in areas of high-traffic noise (with loudness equal to that of a dishwasher or raised voices) have elevated stress-hormone levels, blood pressure, and heart rates. Girls tend to be affected more than boys, becoming less motivated and more prone to depression.

Surrounding oneself with noise is sometimes a choice. It isn't unusual for some people to turn on a radio or TV as soon as they wake up in the morning. Half of America's homes have three or more TVs, and at least one in each household is on for more than eight hours a day! On average, Americans watch TV for almost five hours a day: in the period of a week, this adds up to one entire day dedicated to TV; in a year, that amounts to well over two months!

Silence is becoming endangered—but it is important for your mental and physical health. Silence helps you think more clearly, get a better perspective, and reduce stress. You can see why it's becoming popular to take a day- or weeklong "media fast." I like to go into silence on purpose. It's a practice called *Noble Silence,* and you'll practice it during this week.

○ ○

Initially, as you go into silence, whether for a short meditation period or for a longer time, you'll probably notice that your internal dialogue is even more turbulent and you become more aware of your incessant thoughts. This is a state called the "monkey mind" (which we discussed briefly in Week Two). *I'll be happier in a minute, or when this or that happens.* A sense of urgency or anxiety may come up or you may get fixated on a thought.

You've been practicing becoming aware of your thoughts, so now you can let them arise and dissolve without letting them pull you in different directions or longer conversations. This awareness eventually quiets down your monkey mind, and you begin to experience the stillness of your own soul. This week you can practice *Noble Silence* for a whole or half day, or for an entire weekend. You might be amazed by what happens when there is nothing to do or distract yourself with.

I've had various experiences in this silence, from feeling restless and bored to having lots of thoughts or songs stuck my head. Sometimes there would be numbness, extreme amounts of pain, or some emotional turbulence that turned into blissful peace and contentment. I might feel waves of compassion for all living things, or plan menus, or redecorate a room in my mind. Sometimes I'd feel trapped, then feel unbounded and interconnected; or I'd notice the slightest sound or feel the slightest change in air temperature. There were times I never wanted to stop the immersion into the silence, and times I never wanted to do it again.

There's a moment of grace that arises in the practice of silence. It can happen in or out of meditation. This is when time dissolves into an everlasting present moment. There's a sense that I already have everything I need, and am complete and perfect. The very act of breathing, walking, drinking tea, or chewing is wondrous. There's a communion with all that exists. As I sit outside, I can delight at the offerings—the breeze meeting my skin or a fly buzzing in my ear. Each moment is profound; and sometimes, if I'm lucky, everything becomes one. The tree is me. The squirrel is me. The vast, boundless sky is me. Although they're only words on a page now, these experiences have been very real, giving me a profound sense of interconnection, something wild and gorgeous. I step away from everything I'm certain about.

Exercises and Practices to Cultivate Nourishment

Noble Silence

Noble Silence is a commitment to take a certain amount of time to simply *be* and keep silent, purposely withdrawing from activities that take your attention outside yourself. As you maintain an inner focus, you become aware of thoughts, impulses, and emotions as they arise. Your prejudices and habits of mind will become illuminated. And rather than being swept up by them, bear witness to them. Whether in activity or in meditation, this practice sharpens your senses and makes you more self-aware, bringing you greater wisdom and insight.

When you're in *Noble Silence,* you unplug. You stop speaking, listening to music, watching television or movies, writing, or reading; and you even stop looking in the mirror at the image people recognize as "you." You may feel an intense need to say something to someone or communicate while in silence, whether through writing or gesturing, but refrain from giving in to these impulses. Instead, pay attention to yourself. This practice of silence is a doorway through which you connect with your soul to become the witness to the perfect flow of your own life.

A Personal Retreat

This week continue your daily meditations, and if you can, set aside some time to give yourself a mini–meditation retreat. (I heard someone say once, "We shouldn't call it a *retreat*; it's an *advance.*") Even though a half day, full day, or one week of unplugging from your virtual world and delving into silence may seem like a long time, I encourage you to give it a try this week.

Schedule your retreat as you would any vacation. Let people know that you're unavailable. Get everything ready in advance. Be sure you don't have to go out for food or any errands during the period that you're going on your retreat. Remain in *Noble Silence* throughout the allotted time.

A Personal Retreat gives your entire nervous system the deep rest it needs to rejuvenate and support a soul-centered life. It's also a great way to start new habits like eating for maximum digestion and going to sleep earlier to shift your rhythms and reduce stress. To begin your retreat, unplug your phone and shut all electronics off. Maintain present-moment awareness and a beginner's mind.

Here's a suggested schedule for a full day:

— Get up at sunrise, then slowly and mindfully take a shower or bath. Do your morning routine with total awareness.

— Get dressed slowly.

— Set an intention for the day,

— Sit comfortably, then scan and relax your body.

— Practice *Long, Slow, Deep Breathing* for 3 to 5 minutes.

— Meditate in silence with focus on your breath or a mantra for 20 to 30 minutes, sitting quietly for at least 2 minutes after the period.

— Slowly and mindfully fix and eat breakfast.

— Clean up mindfully.

— Go outside and practice *Walking with Awareness* for 10 to 30 minutes.

— Upon your return, sit comfortably and practice the *Heart-Centered Breath* meditation for 3 to 5 minutes.

— Put your attention on your intention, then let it go. If you don't know what you want, practice a *Self-Inquiry* before you go into meditation. Ask yourself, "Who am I?" and "What is my heart's desire?" a few times while keeping your attention on your heart. Be still and listen.

— Practice the *Sitting Meditation* or the *Mantra Meditation* for 20 minutes. When finished, lie down and do the *Loving Your Body* exercise as you relax, palms up, for 10 minutes. When you are complete, slowly get up.

— Mindfully and with present-moment awareness prepare your lunch. Eat lunch slowly and mindfully as in the *Delectable Eating* practice.

— Clean up or do household chores mindfully and slowly: you can do dishes, sweep, fold clothes, or anything else that doesn't require electronics or reading for 30 to 60 minutes.

— Before dinner, sit comfortably for meditation, practicing *Loving Kindness* for 10 to 15 minutes, then the *Mantra Meditation* or *Sitting Meditation* for 15 to 20 minutes.

— Prepare dinner and eat it mindfully.

— Clean up with awareness.

— After dinner, go outside and do at least 10 minutes of *Walking with Awareness,* or if you prefer, *Walking Without Labels.*

— Get to bed by 10. Before bed, practice the *Gratitude Meditation.*

Schedule of Practices and Exercises

Week Eight: Suggested Daily Practices	
AM	Mantra or Sitting Meditation: 15 Minutes
PM	Mantra or Sitting Meditation: 15 Minutes

Additional Awareness Exercises	
Anytime	Noble Silence
A day this week	A Personal Retreat

Insights for Success

Throughout this final week of your program, pay attention to how you eat and when you sleep, and discover ways to align your habits to create a nourishing life. Remember to surround yourself with silence whenever appropriate to give your nervous system a break. Keep up your daily sitting meditation practice, whether your focus is on your breath or a mantra. Add any of the additional exercises and practices that have nurtured you throughout the weeks.

I realize there's a lot to remember from what you've learned in the 8-week program, so to make it easy for you, I've compiled a list of reminders for how to take excellent care of yourself every day after you've completed this program. Following these suggestions will ensure that you are always living a soul-centered life:

— Sit in silence and meditate for at least 30 minutes each day. (You can do it all at once or in two periods of 15 minutes each, as you did in this program.) This clears the channels of communication between you and your soul and helps you "re-source" your energy.

— Become more self-aware. Pay attention to your breath and body. Get in the habit of asking yourself, "How do I feel right now?"

— Slow it down. Do one thing at a time. Whether taking a shower, driving, or walking, break the habit of rushing. It's easier to enjoy your own life in that way.

— If you feel stressed, bring your attention right here and now, to the present moment. Allow yourself to feel how you feel, emotionally and physically, and give yourself some slow deep breaths. The body and the breath are both anchors to the present moment.

— Approach life with a beginner's mind. Don't assume others see what you see or feel what you feel. Let yourself be present with what is, and maintain a childlike curiosity. With an open mind, wisdom is found everywhere.

— Walk in nature daily, without talking on your cell phone. Notice the colors, textures, shapes, temperature, sounds, aromas, space, light, shadows, movement, stillness, and presence of nature as it sweetly meets your senses.

— When you notice that you regularly have the same stressful thought over and over, ask yourself: "Who would I be if I didn't believe that thought?" and "How would I live my life without the thought?" You might find a moment of peace.

— Notice how you feel when you hear about someone else's success. Practice being sympathetically joyful for that person.

— Be kind to yourself; say nice things to yourself and mean them. Practice loving your body.

— Give yourself permission to do or receive what nurtures you, whether it's singing, listening to music, dancing, volunteering, watching funny movies, painting, journaling, cooking, being with friends, playing or watching sports, gardening, taking a nap, walking the dog, deep breathing, prayer, helping others, or allowing others to help you.

— Say what you mean. Say yes when you mean yes, and no when you mean no. You'll make things easier for yourself and everyone else, and you'll save a lot of time.

— When faced with a choice, pay attention to how you feel; notice the sensations in your body. Use your inner compass and live with integrity. There's no need to manipulate yourself. Ask yourself, "Is it a yes or a no, or a yum or a yuck?" Move toward the yums and away from the yucks.

— When making a choice or taking action, relinquish your need for approval from others. You are the wise one. You usually do know best. You are soul-centered.

— Be "in circle" with those you love. Be present for another as they are interacting with you. Become more comfortable with silence.

— Ask yourself what you really want, and then simply listen to the answer as it comes from within. In my experience, the answer always meets the question, even though it isn't often immediate.

— Accentuate the positive. Pay true attention to what you say you are paying attention to. Whatever you put your attention on grows, so make a shift if it isn't nourishing.

— Practice receiving what others and the universe provide.

— Each night before you go to bed, appreciate your life and be grateful for that which supports your life. Or simply say, "Thank you." Then you can say it again when you wake up!

— Nourish your body and mind and spirit. Choose nourishing food, environments, and relationships. Eat slowly and mindfully. Go to bed early to get a good night's sleep every night.

— Whether for an hour, a day, or a weekend, treat yourself to an extended period of silence. Unplug from everything and give yourself a mini–meditation retreat.

You have all the practices and exercises you need to live a soul-centered life, so enjoy yourself and your soul-full life! You are never evolving or transforming too soon. You are prepared, you are ready, and it's happening right on time. And remember, meditation only works if you do it.

Overview of the 8 Weeks of Practices by Week

Week	AM	Mins	PM	Mins
1	Breath Awareness	15	Body Awareness	15
2	Long, Slow, Deep Breathing	3	Body Awareness	3
			Sitting Meditation	12
	Sitting Meditation	12		
3	Long, Slow, Deep Breathing	3	Walking Without Labels	3
			Sitting Meditation	12
	Sitting Meditation	12		
4	Long, Slow, Deep Breathing	3	Loving Your Body Exercise	5
	Sitting Meditation	12	Sitting Meditation	10

Week	AM	Mins	PM	Mins
5	Self-Inquiry: Who Am I?	3	Walking with Awareness	5
	Sitting Meditation	12	Mantra Meditation	10
6	Heart-Centered Breath	2	Mantra or Sitting Meditation	15
	Self-Inquiry: Who Am I?	3		
	Mantra or Sitting Meditation	10		
7	Heart-Centered Breath	2	Mantra or Sitting Meditation	15
	Self-Inquiry: What is My Heart's Desire?	3		
	Mantra or Sitting Meditation	10		
8	Mantra or Sitting Meditation	15	Mantra or Sitting Meditation	15

Additional Awareness Exercises by Week

Week		Week	
1	Slow down	5	Cultivating Sympathetic Joy
	Mindful Living Exercises		
2	Peacefinder Exercises	6	Listening with Love
	Body Awareness		
	Breath Awareness		
3	Delectable Eating	7	Embodying Your Beauty
	Body Awareness		Walking in a Wonderful World
	Three Beginner's Mind Moments		Gratitude Meditation
4	Don't Believe Everything You Think	8	Noble Silence
	Loving Your Body		A Personal Retreat
	Loving Kindness Meditation		
	Affirming Your Perfection		

AFTERWORD

Meditation is an essential travel partner on your journey of personal transformation. Meditation connects you with your soul, and this connection gives you access to your intuition, your heartfelt desires, your integrity, and the inspiration to create a life you love—a *soul-centered* life.

Throughout the program you learned many practices and exercises to transform the way you live. By now these practices have created new habits, such as paying attention to the moment at hand, feeling your feelings, being less judgmental, loving yourself, being compassionate, communicating authentically, and speaking your truth.

These past 8 weeks have been filled with deep transformational meditation and self-awareness practices, and by embarking on this program, you have made a commitment to change your life. Your brain quite possibly rewired itself, and your circuits are now altered in order to support a new self-awareness, a reduced stress response, and an increased compassion for yourself and others. Keep up your meditation practice; it's a great way to be happy.

Meditation is good medicine, but it's more like taking a vitamin than an aspirin. Ideally, you use it every day as a way to prevent a problem or issue from arising, not as a way to "fix" yourself when you're stressed. Don't use meditation as an escape from your real life or responsibilities; instead, use it as a tool to help you navigate your life in a responsive and mindful way. In an interview, the Dalai Lama suggested that people should meditate "not for the next life, not for heaven, but for your day-to-day well-being."

Some major changes may already be showing up in your daily life, and that can be pretty exciting. Sometimes all the changes, insights, and sense of expansion can be overwhelming, like nothing you've felt before, and you might find yourself uncomfortable with this new state of openness and looking for ways to feel more grounded. Emotional issues may come up that you would rather escape from. You may fall back into old patterns and habits that are not nourishing to you. If this happens, don't be too hard on yourself. With awareness, change can become comfortable.

Years of meditation practice have transformed the way I see myself and the world. One way I maintain that transformation is to remember my personal credo: *Faith, patience, and grace.* You may want to adopt my words or develop your own as a touchstone.

Faith is a deep trust that the universe and life itself are on my side—and they're on your side, too. Life is unfolding perfectly for each one of us. I trust that every desire I have will ultimately result in an outcome best suited for me and all others, in perfect timing. This, of course, requires patience.

Patience is doing my practices: staying in the present moment, meditating, taking care of myself, feeling my emotions, paying attention to my body, listening to my intuition, saying yes and no authentically, inquiring into thoughts that cause me pain or discomfort, choosing nourishing experiences and relationships, giving and receiving freely, finding things to be grateful for, and spending time in silence. This leads to grace.

Grace is a wondrous communion with the creative intelligence that totally surprises and delights me. It's the unfolding perfection that completely supports each one of us on our heartfelt path.

I wish you faith, patience, and grace, along with peace and inspiration, as you journey along this path toward a soul-centered life.

○ ○ ○

RESOURCES FOR ADDITIONAL SUPPORT AND INSPIRATION

Books

Bolte Taylor, Jill. *My Stroke of Insight*. Viking, 2008.

Chopra, Deepak. *Perfect Health: The Complete Mind/Body Guide (revised and updated)*. Three Rivers Press, 2001

Chopra, Deepak. *Quantum Healing: Exploring the Frontiers of Mind/Body Medicine*. Bantam Books, 1989

Chopra, Deepak. *The Seven Spiritual Laws of Success: A Practical Guide to the Fulfillment of Your Dreams*. Amber-Allen Publishing and New World Library, 1994

Ford, Debbie. *The Secret of the Shadow: The Power of Owning Your Whole Story*. Harper Collins, 2002

Hanh, Thich Nhat. *The Miracle of Mindfulness: An Introduction to the Practice of Meditation*. Beacon Press, 1975

Hanh, Thich Nhat. *Peace Is Every Step: The Path of Mindfulness in Everyday Life*. Bantam Books, 1991

Hesse, Hermann. *Siddhartha*. Penguin Classics, 2005 (originally published in 1922)

Katie, Byron, with Stephen Mitchell. *Loving What Is: Four Questions That Can Change Your Life*. Harmony Books, 2002

Pert, Candace B. *Molecules of Emotion: The Science Behind Mind-Body Medicine.* Touchstone, 1999

Rosenberg, Marshall. *Non Violent Communication: A Language of Life.* PuddleDancer Press, 2003

Shearer, Alistair, and Peter Russell (translators). *Upanishads.* Harmony, 2003

Shimoff, Marci. *Happy for No Reason.* Free Press, 2008.

Tolle, Eckhart. *A New Earth: Awakening to Your Life's Purpose.* Penguin, 2005

Tolle, Eckhart. *The Power of Now: A Guide to Spiritual Enlightenment.* New World Library, 1999

Zimmerman, Jack, and Virginia Coyle. *The Way of Council.* Bramble Books, 1996

Zukav, Gary. *The Seat of the Soul.* Simon & Schuster, 1989

CDs (available at McLeanMeditation.com and Amazon.com)

Meditate: Guided Meditations with Sarah McLean
Soul Meditations: Guided Meditations to Transform Your Life

Websites

www.McLeanMeditation.com
www.SedonaMeditation.com

o o o

ACKNOWLEDGMENTS

My deepest gratitude goes out to all whose love, support, and talents have turned the thought of this book into a reality. I am especially grateful to my devoted and delightful husband, Marty; my clear-thinking, multitalented editor Nancy Marriott; my fun-loving agent, Bill Gladstone at Waterside; and everyone at Hay House—including my editor Shannon Littrell for giving me the gift of her keen editorial eye, and Reid Tracy who took a chance on me.

I am blessed by and thankful for my friends and support team, including Melissa Karolides, Victoria and Peter Nelson, Brent BecVar, Leanne Dubois, Jeanna and Mike Zelin, Colette Baron-Reid, Marc Lindeman, David, June and Catherine Chiesa, Kathy Zavada, Carol Studenka, Eric Long, Eric Larson, Dennis Andres, Rachel and Joe Sacco, Sandy Trudel, Pamela Fallon, David Marsden, Ray and Mary Hughes, Sandy Muse, Isaac Gomez, Susan Campbell, Jennifer McLean, Joe Vella, Apryl Rahbari, Barrie Brian, Susan Johnson, Deborah Morrison, Debby Doyle, Kevin Kammer, Amanda Rignalda, Mary Cravets, Terri McMahon, Mike Shingleton, Donna Lyn Tamaroff, Hale Dwoskin, Amy Edwards, Deidre Raven, Tricia and Dan Garland, Maura and Ed Mark, Isaac Hernandez, Alisa Gray, Charlotte Howard, Susan and Eric Henkels, Lilou Mace, Joyce Duchscherer, Susan Riley, Zeffi Kefala, Sherab Khandro, Dennis Harness, Jim Bishop, Debra Beck, Joe Villegas, Kelley Alexander, Dean Taraborelli, Linda Birse, Barbara Litrell,

Herb Deer, Sharon Hooper, Candace Beringer, Lisa Dahl; and everyone at Ken's Creekside, India Palace, and APizza Heaven.

To my family who loves and believes in me: my mother, Mary; my brother, Winston; my nieces, Courtney and Maddie; and my nephew, Winston III. And to my sweet kids by marriage, Danielle and Sasha, and Miss Sheena. And to my clever dogs, Rudolph and Gigi.

Special thanks to Deepak Chopra, David Simon, Debbie Ford, Arielle Ford, Byron Katie, Stephen Mitchell, Seisen Saunders, Tenshin Fletcher, Gary Zukav, and Linda Francis, whose support and encouragement over the years has been invaluable.

My heartfelt gratitude goes to these wise ones who inspire me from afar, though I keep them close to my heart: Mata Amritanandamayi, Thich Nhat Hanh, and the Dalai Lama.

Most important, to all my students who have participated in my meditation programs and retreats throughout the years, among them Roland, Liz, Carol, Hazel, Judy, Ken, Monica, Ann, Amy, Allison, Wesley, Jim, Humbelina, Karen, Kim, Julia, Cat, Ely, Kendra, Sonja, Sharon, Don, Damien, Marion, Suzanne, Dee, and Stacy. I am deeply grateful for each one of you for your courage to share your stories, trials, and successes; and for your dedication to living a soul-centered life.

And finally, to my readers: I am inspired by you and your commitment to finding peace and transforming your life. I am honored you have chosen this book to accompany you on your journey.

◉ ◉ ◉

ABOUT THE AUTHOR

 **Sarah McLean**, an inspiring contemporary meditation teacher, makes meditation accessible to everyone. She has spent much of her life exploring the world's spiritual and mystic traditions, and has worked with some of today's great teachers, including Deepak Chopra, Byron Katie, Debbie Ford and Gary Zukav. She's lived and studied in a Zen Buddhist monastery, meditated in ashrams and temples throughout India and the Far East, spent time in Afghan refugee camps, bicycled the Silk Route from Pakistan to China, trekked the Golden Triangle in Southeast Asia and taught English to Tibetan Buddhist Nuns in Dharamsala.

Sarah is the founding director of the Sedona Meditation Training Company and The McLean Meditation Institute, educational companies offering meditation training, self-discovery retreats and teacher training certification programmes that have transformed thousands of lives, and have earned her the praise of her peers and students.

www.SedonaMeditation.com
www.McLeanMeditationInstitute.com

NOTES

NOTES

NOTES

NOTES

NOTES

NOTES

NOTES

NOTES

Hay House Titles of Related Interest

YOU CAN HEAL YOUR LIFE, the movie,
starring Louise L. Hay & Friends
(available as a 1-DVD program and
an expanded 2-DVD set)
Watch the trailer at: **www.LouiseHayMovie.com**

THE SHIFT, the movie,
starring Dr Wayne W. Dyer
(available as a 1-DVD program and
an expanded 2-DVD set)
Watch the trailer at: **www.DyerMovie.com**

○ ○

AWAKENING THE LUMINOUS MIND:
Tibetan Meditations for Inner Peace and Joy,
by Tenzin Wangyal Rinpoche (available June 2012)

HEAL YOUR BODY, by Louise L. Hay

JUICY JOY: 7 Simple Steps to Your Glorious, Gutsy Self,
by Lisa McCourt

MAXIMISE YOUR HEALTH WITH THE BLOOD TYPE DIET:
A Revolutionary Plan to Achieve Optimum Wellness, by Dr James D'Adamo

TRANSCENDENTAL MEDITATION: The Essential Teachings of Maharishi
Mahesh Yogi. Revised and Updated for the 21st Century, by Jack Forem
(available September 2012)

WHO WOULD YOU BE WITHOUT YOUR STORY?
Dialogues with Byron Katie, by Byron Katie

All of the above are available at your local bookstore,
or may be ordered by contacting Hay House (see next page).

○ ○

We hope you enjoyed this Hay House book. If you'd like
to receive our online catalog featuring additional
information on Hay House books and products,
or if you'd like to find out more about the
Hay Foundation, please contact:

Hay House UK, Ltd., 292B Kensal Rd., London W10 5BE
Phone: 0-20-8962-1230 • *Fax:* 0-20-8962-1239
www.hayhouse.co.uk • **www.hayfoundation.org**

○ ○

Published and distributed in the United States by: Hay House, Inc., P.O. Box
5100, Carlsbad, CA 92018-5100 • *Phone:* (760) 431-7695 or (800) 654-5126 (760) •
Fax: 431-6948 or (800) 650-5115 **www.hayhouse.com**®

Published and distributed in Australia by: Hay House Australia Pty. Ltd., 18/36
Ralph St., Alexandria NSW 2015 • *Phone:* 612-9669-4299 • *Fax:* 612-9669-4144 •
www.hayhouse.com.au

Published and distributed in the Republic of South Africa by:
Hay House SA (Pty), Ltd., P.O. Box 990, Witkoppen 2068
Phone/Fax: 27-11-467-8904 • www.hayhouse.co.za

Published in India by: Hay House Publishers India, Muskaan Complex, Plot No.
3, B-2, Vasant Kunj, New Delhi 110 070 • *Phone:* 91-11-4176-1620 • *Fax:* 91-11-
4176-1630 • www.hayhouse.co.in

Distributed in Canada by: Raincoast, 9050 Shaughnessy St., Vancouver, B.C.
V6P 6E5 • *Phone:* (604) 323-7100
Fax: (604) 323-2600 • www.raincoast.com

○ ○

Take Your Soul on a Vacation

Visit **www.HealYourLife.com**® to regroup, recharge, and reconnect with your
own magnificence. Featuring blogs, mind-body-spirit news, and life-changing
wisdom from Louise Hay and friends.

Visit **www.HealYourLife.com** today!

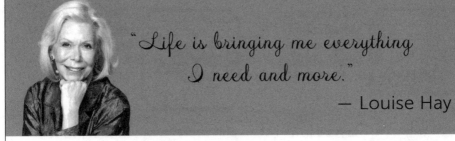

JOIN THE HAY HOUSE FAMILY

As the leading self-help, mind, body and spirit publisher in the UK, we'd like to welcome you to our family so that you can enjoy all the benefits our website has to offer.

 **EXTRACTS** from a selection of your favourite author titles

 **COMPETITIONS, PRIZES & SPECIAL OFFERS** Win extracts, money off, downloads and so much more

 **LISTEN** to a range of radio interviews and our latest audio publications

 **CELEBRATE YOUR BIRTHDAY** An inspiring gift will be sent your way

 **LATEST NEWS** Keep up with the latest news from and about our authors

 **ATTEND OUR AUTHOR EVENTS** Be the first to hear about our author events

 **iPHONE APPS** Download your favourite app for your iPhone

 **HAY HOUSE INFORMATION** Ask us anything, all enquiries answered

join us online at **www.hayhouse.co.uk**

 292B Kensal Road, London W10 5BE
T: 020 8962 1230 E: info@hayhouse.co.uk